D1520871

DEATH

— ALONG THE —

NATCHEZ TRACE

Josh Foreman and Ryan Starrett

THE
History
PRESS

Published by The History Press
Charleston, SC
www.historypress.com

First published 2022

Manufactured in the United States

ISBN 9781467149778

Library of Congress Control Number: 2021950618

Notice: The information in this book is true and complete to the best of our knowledge. It is offered without guarantee on the part of the authors or The History Press. The authors and The History Press disclaim all liability in connection with the use of this book.

To Joseph Padraic and Penelope Rose O. Starrett. If I had been given the power to design the ideal children, I would have fallen short of you two. Thank you for everything, particularly for going up and down, up and down, up and down the Natchez Trace for this book, from Natchez's Hotel Vue to the Nashville Zoo and every site and grave in between.

—Ryan

And to Keeland, Genevieve and "Little Rupert," the kids who keep life loud and lively.

—Josh

CONTENTS

CONTENTS

FOREWORD

The mystique of the Natchez Trace was born in stories told around campfires on the historic road. Southeastern tribes and settlers alike created narrative histories by selecting significant facts from their travels and spinning them into tales. The strange, the mysterious and the larger-than-life drew the listeners' attention and branded stories into memories.

Even after years of research and writing about the Natchez Trace, I find it difficult to separate fact from fiction or extraordinary truths from the elements added as part of the storyteller's art. Early Natchez Trace historians who attempted to create a scholarly method of interpreting the history of the road by rejecting every story "my grandpappy told me" left us with only half truths. Sometimes an ancestor's oral history, recorded years later, proved more reliable than a two-hundred-year-old document written with limited knowledge or improper motives.

In this collection, Ryan Starrett and Josh Foreman have selected stories that draw the reader into the dark canebrakes and along the foggy swamps of the legendary Natchez Trace. They show how the road tested each traveler, producing both heroes and villains. Only the strong and the clever survived. In focusing on that challenge, the authors uncover the essence of the legend that still intrigues—human nature tested to its extremes.

Historians and those who grew up along the Natchez Trace often are so invested in their own versions of Trace history that they insist that all others are in error. I understand their passion. But while I may differ from these authors in my interpretation of the death of Meriwether Lewis, their perspective is equally worthy of study. We all must accept that none of us has a perfect looking glass into the past.

As you prepare to explore the historic Natchez Trace, sit back around the figurative campfire as Street and Foreman tell its stories with the art of early storytellers. Some chapters are familiar tales retold from a different perspective, while others are highlighted here for the first time. Either way, the tales will immerse you into the mythical, legendary gauntlet early travelers survived to help create what we now know as the American South.

—TONY L. TURNBOW

PREFACE

I write at eighty-five for the same reasons that impelled me to write at forty-five; I was born with a passionate desire to communicate, to organize experience, to tell tales that dramatize the adventures which readers might have had.
I have been that ancient man who sat by the campfire at night and regaled the hunters with imaginative recitations about their prowess. The job of an apple tree is to bear apples. The job of a storyteller is to tell stories, and I have concentrated on that obligation.
—James Michener

The Natchez Trace is a trail of animal necessity and human ingenuity. It is a path of peace and prosperity as well as war and destruction. It is a way in the wilderness that connects two cultural capitals. It is the four-hundred-plus-mile stretch of land connecting Nashville and Natchez.

The Trace began as a prehistoric game trail used by wild animals navigating virgin forests. It was later used by pre–European contact Indians who later became the Natchez, Choctaw, Chickasaw, Creek and Cherokee tribes. It saw its heyday from circa 1790 to 1820, when Kaintucks decided that it was cheaper to travel up the old Indian trail to Nashville (rather than pay for boat fees back to their northern homes). When the steamship made traveling the Trace impractical, it endured. However, less traffic meant fewer towns between Natchez and Nashville. It also signaled the end of the age of stands (hostels along the Trace). On the eve of World War II, President Roosevelt signed legislation to complete a parkway roughly paralleling the

Old Trace. Today, the 444-mile Parkway is still traveled by hikers, bikers, motorists, locals, tourists and history aficionados.

Billions of transients made the Trace a layover on their yearly migrations (from Canada, à la passenger pigeons) or New Orleans (via the Kaintucks). The outcasts of society (like Samuel Mason), the feted of society (like Bernie Ebbers) and society itself (like President Jackson) made the Trace and its environs their abode. Most used the Trace as a means to move from one destination to the next (the buffalo seeking the salt licks of central Tennessee and John Swanton, the mailman charged with delivering the Nashville mail to Natchez and vice versa), but many chose to build their permanent abodes along the ancient trail (see James Robertson, the founder of Nashville, and Daniel Burnett, owner of the stand Grindstone Ford). Countless died wrapped in the arms of the Trace's abundant foliage, swamps and forests. They died by alligator, snake, mosquito, fire, bullet, starvation, tornado, battle and suicide. But many more used the Trace, abused the Trace, nourished the Trace, rebuilt the Trace and made a life along the Trace.

The Natchez Trace is a mysterious, haunted, beautiful piece of Americana. Its stories, recorded and unrecorded, have nourished generation upon generation of storytellers.

The following book is a collection of a few dozen tales of the Natchez Trace. Aside from the last chapter, we have tried our damnedest to root every chapter, every vignette, in verifiable history. We hope that you enjoy the following tales. More importantly, we hope you explore the Natchez Trace—in person or via your own research. It is an invitation to get to know the Natchez Trace we grew up on, the Natchez Trace we still reside near, the Natchez Trace we love.

Chapter 1

FIRST CONTACT

BOWS, BROADSWORDS AND DEAD ALL AROUND

Spanish River Flight, 1542

Moonlight fell on the body of Hernando de Soto. The Indians could not be allowed to get the body, or else the conquistador would become disassembled. The Indians would love to string his parts from the branches of some cursed tree. No, De Soto would instead find his grave among the gars and catfish, nineteen fathoms deep.

His men took one last look at their *adelantado* and then slotted him into a carved-out oak log. They nailed planks over the body and sank it in the middle of the Mississippi River, somewhere off northeast Louisiana. De Soto's dream of finding gold in the Southeast sank along with him. Soon, the men of his expedition would come to an agreement: after three years traversing this land, they would get the hell out. Luis de Moscoso would lead them.[1]

The Spaniards traveled west, hoping to reach Mexico overland. But west offered only hunger, privation and guerrilla attacks. The Mississippi, they decided, was their best chance at escape. But in order to travel the river, the 350 Spaniards, whose linen clothes had long ago disintegrated, would need substantial boats. Among them was a master shipbuilder, but they would need to source their shipbuilding supplies from the land around them.

They set about sawing planks from logs, twisting rope and carving oars. They hammered their arquebuses into nails and collected as many Indian blankets as they could to make sails. By the summer of 1543, the men had

The body of Hernando de Soto was slotted into an oak log and sunk in the Mississippi River in the dead of night. Image originally published in *Our Country in Story* (1917). *Internet Archive.*

built seven brigantines and were ready to begin sailing them south, to the ocean and to Mexico.

But the months of shipbuilding had aroused curiosity across the river. There, on the east bank of the Mississippi, a young cacique named Quigaltanqui had surmised that the Spanish would try to escape by the river. Quigaltanqui hated the Spanish and wanted revenge for three years of Spanish raids on Indian villages.

While the Spanish built their ships, Quigaltanqui sent emissaries to the other caciques along the river. The Spanish should not be allowed to leave, he argued; if they never made it out of the Southeast, they wouldn't be able to tell their countrymen what they had seen during their three-year expedition. Maybe they could rid themselves of the "Bearded Ones" forever. The other caciques agreed, and a plan was made to attack the Spanish as soon as they set out on their voyage.[2]

The 350 Spaniards paddled out on July 2, 1543, their seven brigantines powered by fourteen oars each. Tied to the brigantines were canoes carrying a few pigs and 26 tired and scarred horses, all that remained of the Spaniards' once impressive stock of 225 warhorses. For two days, the going was quiet. Then they began to hear singing. Canoes appeared on the river behind them—one hundred canoes. Each canoe was rowed by at least fourteen men. Some carried as many as eighty. The canoes and the men inside were painted wild colors. As the Indians followed the Spaniards, they sang songs and rowed in unison. "The fish will eat you," they sang. "The dogs will eat you. You are cowards."

Hoping to scare off the fleet, Moscoso ordered twenty-five of his men to board their own canoes and attack the pursuing Indians. The Spaniards had few crossbows and no arquebuses, so the attack would be carried out with sword and shield. On land, the attack might have succeeded, but the Spaniards would soon learn that canoe warfare was the Indians' specialty.

When the Spaniards pulled up close to the Indian canoes, many of the Indians dove into the water. Some held the gunwales of their own canoes to steady them, while others swam underneath the Spaniards' boats, grabbing their gunwales and flipping them. The Spaniards wearing armor sank immediately, joining De Soto on the river bottom. The Indians who remained in the canoes attacked furiously with oars and clubs.

The Spaniards on board the brigantines could only watch in horror as their countrymen perished; the river current was too strong to turn the big boats around and offer aid. Only four Spaniards managed to swim back to the brigantines.[3]

Milepost 243.3. *Ryan Starrett.*

13

A great running battle had begun. For the next three days, the Spaniards would not sleep and would not rest; they would only paddle and steer, hoping to leave the territory of Quigaltanqui. And when the battle was over, Quigaltanqui's people—whom the French would know as the Natchez more than 150 years later—would sing songs of their victory.

Reed Arrows and Spanish Steel

When De Soto's expedition of seven hundred disembarked in Southwest Florida in 1539, they carried ashore the European technologies that had helped the Spanish utterly subjugate Indians in the Caribbean, Mexico and South America. De Soto himself had accompanied Francisco Pizarro to Peru and had seen the devastating power of horses, guns, armor and steel when pitted against Indian civilizations.

When the De Soto expedition was fresh and traveling overland, the Spanish sent parties of well-armed cavalry and infantry to explore. Cavalrymen carried lances, and infantrymen specialized in fighting with sword and shield, crossbow or, strangest of all to the Indians, arquebuses,

Drawing of a conquistador from the Richard Erdoes Papers. *Beinecke Library at Yale University.*

the early, muzzle-loaded guns that fired lead balls or stones in great gouts of black smoke.

The Spanish steel proved devastatingly effective against southeastern Indians, who wore little to no armor. About a year and half into their expedition, the Spanish fought a major battle at a fortified Indian village called Mabila. At the start of the battle, one of De Soto's captains, Baltasar de Gallagos, had swung his sword with such power that his Indian adversary was nearly cut in half, from his shoulder down to his bowels.

The Spaniards' crossbows fired heavy, iron-tipped bolts with great power, could be operated in tight quarters and did not require special skill or knowledge to use effectively. Their arquebus muskets were crude and "cannonlike," could weigh as much as fifty pounds and were unreliable and inaccurate—although impressive, with their thunderous discharges. Both crossbows and arquebuses proved far less effective at fighting Indians than swords, lances, horses and war dogs.[4]

Cavalrymen engaging Indians in the open killed them at will with their lances. The Indians did not fight with pikes, the traditional European weapon used to counter cavalry attacks. And the Indians, who could easily outrun Spanish foot soldiers, lost that advantage to horses.[5]

Spanish armor—which included steel helmets and breastplates, shields, chain mail, leather and thick cotton quilt—reduced the effectiveness of Indian arrows, the Indians' preferred means of inflicting death on their enemies. But the incredible power, speed and accuracy of Indian archers meant that many Spaniards still fell victim. Bows were light, portable and inexpensive, and they could be shot five or six times in the time it took to reload a crossbow. And Indians could fire their arrows with such force that they could pierce two layers of Spanish chain mail.[6]

The captain who had cut the warrior nearly in half with his sword was immediately feathered with six or seven arrows from another warrior— striking his armor, the arrows had no effect. Indian arrows were tipped with flint or deer horn or sometimes simply sharpened and hardened by fire. Bow strings were made from deer sinew, and bows were used as deadly clubs when arrows were expended. At Mabila, a well-aimed arrow entered another Spaniard's eye with so much velocity that it exited the back of his head. Indians quickly realized that Spanish armor meant they had to shoot at their enemies' bearded faces. In that battle, eighteen Spaniards perished from arrow wounds to their faces.

In all, eighty-two Spaniards died in the Battle of Mabila. But the number of Indian dead attests to the superiority of Spanish arms and

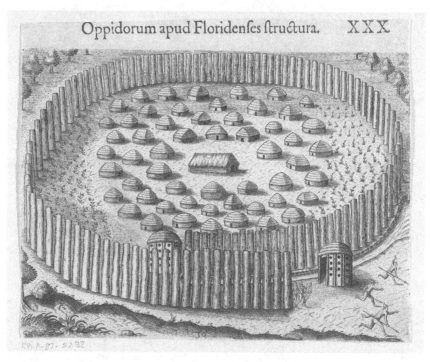

A fortified Indian village in Florida, originally depicted by an anonymous artist in 1591. *Rijksmuseum.*

armor in traditional warfare; the number of Indian casualties numbered in the thousands, with as many as three thousand alone dying to Spanish swordsmen.[7]

While the Spanish prevailed on the open field, Indians were masters of guerrilla warfare, striking at night with fire and arrows and fleeing before the Spanish could mount a defense. Indians learned quickly not only to fire their arrows at Spaniards' faces and other unarmored parts but also to shoot at horses before riders; if the horse died, the Spaniard lost his most effective advantage. The countless guerrilla attacks De Soto's men endured while traveling in the Southeast contributed to the loss of resolve that followed his death.

Indians were vigilant, sleeping beside a strung bow and a dozen arrows. Indian women could wield bows as well as men, as the Spaniards learned at the Battle of Mabila. Centuries of ranged warfare had trained Indians to evade Spanish arquebuses and crossbows. Álvar Núñez Cabeza de Vaca, who had traveled Florida a decade before De Soto with the Narváez expedition, described the tactic: "[B]ending low to the earth, and whilst shot at they move about, speaking and leaping from one point to another, thus avoiding the shafts of their enemies. So effectual is their maneuvering that they can receive very little injury from crossbow or arquebus; they rather scoff at them."[8]

And, of course, the warriors serving Quigaltanqui had mastered river warfare, as the fleeing Spaniards led by Moscoso learned in 1543.

A Narrow Escape

Moscoso's Spaniards were amazed at the speed with which the Indians could travel along the river. The Indians separated their fleet into three groups and moved into battle formation. One group would row down the west bank of the river, past the brigantines, and then swing in front of them. The Indians would unload their bows on the Spanish and then cross to the east side of the river and drop behind. The three groups of Indian canoes took turns encircling the Spanish in this way, loosing a never-ending rain of arrows.

The Spaniards had erected shields of armor and cane mats along the sides of their brigantines. To compensate, Quigaltanqui's warriors fired their arrows high, allowing them to arc down into the boats and reach their targets. The Spaniards could offer no resistance; they possessed as few as one crossbow per boat and no arquebuses. The twenty-six horses riding in the canoes behind the brigantines were wiped out by the constant barrage of Indian arrows, much to the sorrow of the Spaniards, who had relied on them so much in the previous four years.

The Indians, ever the keen judges of their enemies' weaknesses, allowed the Spaniards to rest on the first night of the battle, but only for a moment. Hearing the river go silent behind them, the Spaniards believed that they had finally left Quigaltanqui's territory. It was a ruse—the warriors in the canoes had silently paddled close to the brigantines. The night erupted in war cries, and the attack began anew.

For two more days, Quigaltanqui's warriors followed the Spaniards, firing arrows, attacking any brigantine that became separated from the others and relishing in the fear and desperate paddling of the Spaniards. Finally, the Spaniards passed the borders of Quigaltanqui's kingdom, and the warriors turned their canoes around. The Spaniards eventually made their way to the ocean and to Mexico.[9]

Emerald Mound, milepost 10.3. *Ryan Starrett.*

At some point during the three days of battle, the Spaniards passed the site of the future city of Natchez and the terminus of the Natchez Trace. It is highly possible that Quigaltanqui sat atop a great mound there, orchestrating his attack.

Although no historical record exists, archaeological records indicate that Emerald Mound might have been Quigaltanqui's seat of power. The mound site, which sits on the Trace around ten miles north of Natchez, was a major village and ceremonial center, inhabited by the ancestors of the Natchez at the time De Soto's expedition passed by in 1543. At that time, the main mound formed an enormous platform more than seven hundred feet long and four hundred feet wide and was surrounded by eight smaller mounds. The sheer size of Emerald Mound suggests its importance; the ancestors of the southeastern Indians built only one larger mound during the period, many miles north at the Cahokia site in Illinois.

Although Quigaltanqui's people surely sang songs about their victory over the Spanish for many years, their contact with the Spanish proved to be the beginning of the end for them. By the time the French "rediscovered" the descendants of Quigaltanqui, Emerald Mound had been abandoned, and the once powerful chiefdom had fractured into smaller groups. Diseases brought by Spaniards and their domesticated animals likely played a role in the civilization's decline.[10]

Emerald Mound sits now lopsided and diminished from four centuries of abandonment and erosion. But an apparition still exists there, outside the pages of history and beyond the reach of memory. The ghost stands atop the mound wearing a mantle of marten fur, a white feather plume standing high atop his head. He looks toward the Mississippi, moving his feet in step, remembering forever his victory over the Bearded Ones and shouting forever his own name: *Quigaltanqui! Quigaltanqui!*

Chapter 2

GRAND VILLAGE

A NATCHEZ FUNERAL

The boy walked up to his father, tied a rope around his neck and strangled him to death. The body fell limp to the earth, next to his deceased wife. The boy had ensured that his mother would have a companion in the next world.

The two, husband and wife, were laid side by side in her house. The boy then called for the twelve babies to be brought inside. Twenty-four parents dutifully brought their recently strangled babies and arranged them around the funeral pyre.

When the boy stepped outside, he looked over fourteen people, faces painted red, sitting atop their individual scaffolds, their families standing beneath. Each of their closest kin was holding a knotted cord and screaming a horrible death cry. As the boy watched, the fourteen descended and danced their way to the middle of the square and continued to dance before the house of the dead woman. Then they danced back to and remounted their scaffolds.[11]

THE LAST MONTHS HAD been delightful. It had been the best time since he had arrived in the New World. Hunting, lounging, carousing—lots of carousing.

André Pénicaut had barely been able to contain his joy when, on account of dwindling supplies and horrid conditions in Mobile, Commander Bienville gave fifty Frenchmen permission to go live among the natives for a few months. Pénicaut immediately suggested to a handful of his

A Natchez man in summer dress. Originally published in *Histoire de Louisiane* (1758). *Internet Archive.*

A mother and her daughter. Originally published in *Histoire de Louisiane* (1758). *Internet Archive.*

comrades that they go back to the village of the Natchez. He had been there before and "all but forgot M. de Bienville's instructions because of all the amusements we had. The village of the Natchez is the most beautiful that could be found in Louisiana."[12]

But even more beautiful than the land were the women. "We found it fascinating to watch them dancing during their festivals [in] their pretty white dresses, all of them bareheaded, their long black hair hanging to their knees and as low as the heels on many of them."[13] The dance would begin at sunset when the dry trunk of a dead pine tree was lit, lighting up the entire square in front of the chief's house. The married men and women would dance together until midnight and then escort one another home. Then the fun began. The unmarried boys and girls got the dancing field until sunrise. When they needed a break, a boy would take his dancing partner into the fields beyond the light and "[dance] with her another cotillion *a la Missicipyene.*"

Inevitably, the population of the Natchez would often increase nine months after these dances, which could last a week or more. If a girl found out she was pregnant, she was asked by her parents whether or not she wanted to keep it. If so, she gave birth and was given the child to suckle. If not, she gave birth and the baby was strangled and buried, making her free to dance again.

For the soldiers of Biloxi, a visit to the Natchez was the greatest of blessings. As the French adventurer led his comrades into the village, his heart leaped when he heard the sound of drums. "Everybody in the village was happy because it was the opening of a dance festival." Then, they heard "such frightful howls that we thought the devils had come out of hell just to get to this place and howl." This was going to be a different type of dance.[14]

PÉNICAUT AND HIS COMPANIONS had unwittingly arrived in Grand Village in 1703 days after the death of the chief's sister. He, along with Dumont de Montigny, two decades later, witnessed a Natchez funeral. They are the only two Europeans who recorded the solemnities and festivities of the rite. Like all native peoples, like all human persons, the Natchez developed intricate rites involving care for the dead. In 1725, Dumont recorded:

> As soon as the Great Chief died, his corpse is dressed in his finest clothing, just as if he were alive, and he is laid out upon his bed. He continues to be given food to eat and a pipe to smoke, just as if he were alive and speaking, for nine days. While he is lying in state on his bed, women with young infants at the breast come to offer him their innocents, whom they suffocate and throw down before him as sacrificial victims.[15]

Twenty-two years earlier, André Pénicaut had stumbled on the funeral of the Great Sun's sister. She, like the male chiefs, was also given an elaborate funeral. Her funeral was not unusual. Although the woman almost certainly was not the leader of the tribe (even though Pénicaut did call her a chief), she was the most important woman in the tribe and an honored, indispensable member.

Natchez society contained two classes. Tradition demanded that royal marriages merge the two classes. Furthermore, the succession was matrilineal.[16] So, when a chief died, he was never replaced by one of his own sons. It was always the son of his sister. His sister, after all, was royal by birth, while his wife was chosen from among the lower class. The sister of the Great Sun conceived, carried and raised the next Great Sun. Her husband, by extension, was of little consequence, having come from the lower class himself. Therefore, when his wife died, he was killed as well so as to accompany her to the next world.[17]

As a result, the funeral witnessed by Pénicaut was eerily similar to that seen by Dumont, and both accounts are in conformity with what contemporary scholars know about Natchez funeral rites.

An early depiction of an Indian funeral ceremony in Florida, by Bernard Picart, 1721. *Rijksmuseum.*

Naturels en Hyver

A Natchez man in winter
dress. Originally published
in *Histoire de Louisiane* (1758).
Internet Archive.

HE HAD KNOWN FOR years that when the great
lady died, he would accompany her to the next
world. He had always wanted to live as a hero.
Now he had the chance to die as one.

He glanced out at the heroes of the tribe.
They were easily identified by the tattoos on
their stomachs—a mixture of black, red and
blue—and the suns, snakes and other fierce
drawings covering the entirety of their near-
naked bodies.[18] He had grown up on tales of
daring and bravery. He knew the story of his
ancestors who defeated the armored boatmen
in the Great River.[19] He had heard scores of
tales of wars with rival tribes. He had seen
prisoners brought back to his village and slowly
dispatched to the next world. He had been on
hunts. He had even been on a raid in which
they brought back two prisoners. But, alas, he
had no deed warranting a tattoo.

But he had something only a handful of his tribesmen could claim: the
dignity of dying for the noble lady, the sister of the Great Sun, the mother
of the next Great Sun. He had promised her his life a decade ago. He had
woven the cord that would strangle him with his own hands. Now, his eldest
son stood beneath him chanting and holding that very cord.

The preliminary dancing had begun. He and the thirteen other sacrifices,
all with faces painted the color of blood and carrying shells, descended
their scaffolds and began to dance toward the house of the deceased. They
moved to the beat of drums, maracas and the shrieking of their kin who
followed behind them chanting the death-song. They danced before the
house, across the village and in front of the temple. Then they returned to
their scaffolds. Fifteen minutes later, the process was repeated. This went
on for four days.[20]

THE FUNERALS PÉNICAUT AND Dumont witnessed took place in Grand
Village. The plaza of Grand Village is about one hundred yards long.
On the south side, near St. Catherine Creek, is the mound on which the
house of the chief, or the Great Sun, stood. One hundred yards to the
northeast sits the temple.[21] Father Le Petit, who lived among the Choctaw

and Natchez from 1726 to 1730, described the temple as an "earthen oven, on the back of a tortoise." It was one hundred feet in circumference with a house on top. The roof was decorated with three wooden eagles—red, yellow and white—while the house itself was surrounded by painted stakes with the heads of their enemies slain in battle. Inside the house were baskets filled with the bones of the favorites who had been strangled to death.[22]

Despite being the spiritual center of the Natchez, Grand Village was sparsely populated. Most of the population of their confederation lived in six neighboring villages.[23] Nevertheless, Grand Village held prominence because it was both the residence of the Great Sun and the temple, which housed the sacred fire.

The sacred fire came from the Sun himself. Should its flame ever be extinguished inside the temple, the eight guards who were on duty, along with their wives and children, would be put to death.[24] The temple also contained the bones of the honored dead. Those of the previous chiefs were placed in large oval baskets, along with the bones of those sacrificed to accompany their chief to the next world.

Soon the bones of the Great Sun's mother would join her ancestors.

HIS FINAL DAWN WAS upon him. He glanced over the square and saw the entire village dressed in their best garments. Those condemned to die with him also appeared in their finest garb. Each bowed to the four corners of the earth—the earth they were to leave in just a few hours.

At last, the great woman was brought forth, and the funeral procession began. The litter-bearers began to carry their chieftainess to her final resting place—slowly. They zigzagged back and forth so as to take the longest possible time before reaching the temple. It was her people's final chance to be with their beloved and feared leader.

The fathers of the twelve slain infants led the way, the fourteen living victims just behind. When they got to the center of the square, the fathers threw their children down, and the four men carrying the woman's stretcher walked on top of the corpses. The fathers then gathered their mangled infants, marched forward ten steps and tossed them on the ground again. Again they were stomped on. The process was repeated until the entourage reached the temple and the fathers held only the mutilated remains of their children.

All along, the drums, maracas, rattles and shrieks filled the air. He and the other condemned had joined the procession of death. The dance became

Grand Village, spiritual center of the Natchez. *Ryan Starrett.*

more and more frenzied. Each step, each leap into the air, each pirouette brought him one movement closer to death. He knew it. And still he danced.

He ceased his festive dance only when he reached the base of the temple. Then he and the other victims sat down. He caught his last glimpse of Grand Village as a deerskin cloth was pulled over his head. He smelled the wild skin and then felt it tighten as members of his own family pulled the cords on either side of him. There was a pause, a minute that seemed like an eternity as fear and wonder gripped his soul. And then came a yank from one side that was almost simultaneously countered by a jerk from the other. He fought for air that he could not inhale. The noose grew tighter and tighter. His mind went blank as his body continued to spasm.

Later, his bones were stripped of their skin and placed in a semi-tomb where they would dry for two months before being moved to the temple to lie beside his chieftainess. The chieftainess and her husband, along with the strangled and trampled babies, were placed atop him.

His soul would now join the others in the mass grave on their journey into the great unknown.[25]

Chapter 3

CREATURES OF THE TRACE

ALLIGATORS, SNAKES AND MOSQUITOES

ALLIGATORS

Let those curse it who curse the day, who are prepared to rouse Leviathan.
—*Job 3:8*

Man was not the only deadly danger on the Natchez Trace. Those over whom he was given dominion have continuously refused to accept that status. The beasts of the land have killed many a traveler along the Trace.[26]

Dumont de Montigny, a French colonial officer in early Louisiana, wrote of an all-too-common occurrence for the region's early explorers:

> *A poor soldier from Bayou St John, at a post near the entrance of the bayou where there is only a small corps of guards, was sleeping on the ground in the shade of a tree, and one of these animals caught him by the foot and dragged him to the bottom of the water, where the poor, unfortunate man was eaten as he drowned. The alligator could easily pull this soldier in, since they truly are strong enough to carry off a buffalo drinking water at the edge of a river.[27]*

Today, the swamps along the Trace are filled with alligators. They would have been so two hundred years ago as well. In fact, they would have been more deadly and more lethal prior to their introduction to humans. Kenneth N. Myers explained:

> *Before the advent of European settlers, that is, before guns and bullets, alligators had no natural predators and the bows and arrows of the Native*

This page: Alligators at the Barataria Preserve, Marrero, Louisiana. *Ryan Starrett.*

A submerged American alligator. *Smithsonian's National Zoo & Conservation Biology Institute.*

Americans were practically harmless to them. Consequently, in the 18th
century when the French began settling along the swamps, rivers and lakes
of Louisiana, the older alligators dwarfed even the record setting specimens
of modern times. One might dismiss a single report of a nineteen or twenty
foot alligator as fanciful, but various reports from multiple sources confirm
the enormous size of the animals in that time.[28]

Alligators of similar size would no doubt have inhabited the sparsely traveled swamps of the Trace, where they would have grown to monstrous proportions at the top of the food chain. Needless to say, the lonely traveler making his way through a swamp, or unfortunate enough to be caught beside a flooding river, would be at a distinct disadvantage when it came to survival. Should he lose, his fate would never be known.

As recently as 2019, a massive twelve-foot-long, 672-pound alligator was captured on the Pearl River. The gator was so well armored that Johnny Gray, who captured it with his brother, Joe, was wounded by bullet fragments that ricocheted off the thick hide and tore into his cheek and nose.[29] An even larger alligator was killed near Natchez two years before by Bryan Burnside and his companions. That gator measured fourteen feet and three quarters of an inch and weighed 766.5 pounds.[30] And yet these two recently slain gators pale in comparison with their predecessors. One is left to wonder what Bryan Burnside and the Gray brothers would have to say to Antoine-Simon Le Page du Pratz's three-century-old boast:

Among other things I cannot omit to give an account of a monstrous large
alligator I killed with a musquet ball, as it lay on the bank, about ten feet
above the edge of the water. We measured it, and found it to be nineteen
feet long….M. Mehane told me, he had killed one twenty two feet long.[31]

SNAKES

And I will put enmity between you and the woman, and between your seed
and her seed; he shall bruise you on the head, and you shall bruise him on
the heel.

—*Genesis 3:15*

While death by alligator would be a particularly traumatic way to go, other animals proved to be just as lethal. There are twenty-five species of snakes

John James Audubon's depiction of a rattlesnake attacking a mockingbird nest. *Audubon.org*

along the Trace, three of which are venomous: canebrake rattlesnake, cottonmouth[32] and copperhead.

It is impossible to determine the number of deaths by snakebite during the Trace's history. But it must have been more than a handful, as effective venom antidotes are a relatively recent invention. A snakebite on the Trace often ended in an agonizing death.

An unnamed man in 1848 encountered a rattlesnake when he awoke from a nap while fishing. "The melting eyeballs glared with sparks of fire—there was a movement; I was aroused from a dreamy state; I saw a huge rattlesnake; its gaze was disturbed, and when I heard the hateful rattle sound, the full danger of my situation aroused me, and through all my frame I felt the extremity of terror."[33]

As he watched the rattlesnake, he felt another snake slither over his shoulders and around his neck. The sheer terror of the moment caused him to lose consciousness, certain that death was literally at his throat. When the fortunate man regained consciousness, he found that a kingsnake had crawled over his body to get at the rattler as quickly as possible.[34]

SHORTLY BEFORE RETIRING FOR the evening, Dr. Frank Guedon reached under his carport to scoop a cup of dogfood. He felt a sharp pain and yanked his hand up. A cottonmouth was hanging off his palm just below his middle two fingers and then fell to the ground. Thinking quickly, Guedon killed the snake with a broom and drove with it to Natchez Regional Medical Center.[35]

Six hours later and filled with six vials of antivenom, Guedon was safely back home. Still, the swelling had spread halfway up his arm. "My hand was swollen so bad that I couldn't touch my [forefinger with my thumb]." After an uncomfortable and nauseous day, Guedon recovered.[36] Most snakebite victims do, if they can get medical attention within two hours.[37] And if they can get antivenom.

IN 1866, THE *NATCHEZ Democrat* promoted a new antidote for all snake bites:

> *The following antidote for snake poison was handed us on the street a day or two since, for publication. We will vouch for its efficacy—though we have never used it—as we know the gentleman to be most reliable. See what he says about it:*
>
> *10 Grains of Iodide of Potassium*
> *30 Grains of Iodide*
> *1 Ounce Water as Solvent*
> *The above is no humbug or quackery. It is an infallible cure....*[O]*ne drop of the antidote is said to render the bite of the most deadly serpent harmless.*[38]

The rattlesnake has fascinated the imagination of man ever since the two came into contact, and for obvious reasons. Three to six feet long, powerful and beautiful, the "gentleman" snake is equipped with rattles that vibrate as a warning to unwary travelers. The annals of the early explorers to Mississippi are filled with references to this charming, lethal snake.

But it is the other two venomous cousins—the cottonmouth and the copperhead—that do the most harm up and down the Trace. Whereas a rattlesnake tends to be nonconfrontational and will likely give plenty of warning before a strike, the copperhead will coil up and not move. A person walking in its territory runs the risk of being bitten before he even sees his attacker.[39] With an even more venomous punch, the cottonmouth has the added danger of being a powerful swimmer, acclimated to swamps, lakes and slow-moving rivers—the very type of waters that dot the Natchez Trace.

While persons like Dr. Guedon and the unnamed newspaper contributor were lucky to survive and tell of their encounters with a venomous snake, others along the Trace were not so fortunate. Unfortunately, there is just no way to determine the number of fatalities when so many solitary travelers traversed the snake-infested Natchez Trace when the closest stand was, at best, twenty miles distant.

MOSQUITOES

They had tails with stingers like scorpions, which had power to injure people for five months.
—Revelation 9:10

Far more deadly than the alligator or snake was the most common and lethal animal on the Natchez Trace: the diminutive mosquito.

One of the earliest settlers in the Deep South, Ursuline nun Marie Hachard, wrote home describing these tiny creatures: "Mosquitoes, little animals....They cause blisters and painful itching. They take away the skin, and then ulcers come when one scratches. The animals sting with such force that we had our faces and hands covered with their marks, but, happily, these insects appear only after the sun goes down. They appear the next day at sunset."[40]

A mere annoyance at first, it would take centuries for people to realize exactly how deadly this creature could be. Yellow fever struck especially hard in the Deep South every few years. Every summer carried with it the

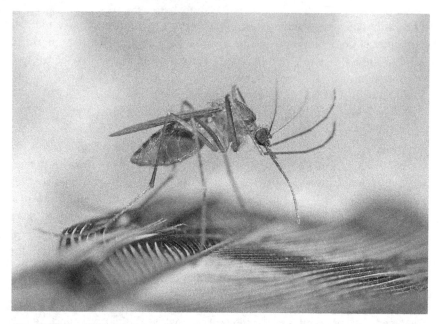

Above: A black-tailed mosquito, native to the Southeast, feeds on a blue jay. *Centers for Disease Control and Prevention.*

Opposite: Cypress Swamps, milepost 122. *Ryan Starrett.*

threat of another epidemic. The 1878 epidemic was particularly lethal, as it killed more than eighteen thousand Americans—most were residents of the South. The communities along the Mississippi River and Natchez Trace—areas prone to pools of stagnant water and mosquitoes—seemed like death zones.

A few days after being bitten by an infected mosquito, a person begins to feel flu-like symptoms. He will likely recover, temporarily. And then the real suffering begins. He begins to vomit black blood, and his liver and kidneys begin to fail. The skin turns yellow, and the victim is usually dead within two weeks.

Perhaps just as awful is the fact that family and friends are basically helpless. The origins of yellow fever are not known, and the only treatment was to alleviate as much pain as possible and pray that their loved one would be one of the lucky ones.

Civic leaders often instituted strict quarantines causing social life and business to come to a screeching halt—a total government shutdown. A *Washington Post* article from September 9, 1878, reported:

In New Orleans, Vicksburg and Memphis, as well as the smaller towns of Holly Springs, Grenada, Port Gibson, Canton, Greenville, Brownsville, Baton Rouge and Delhi, all business is entirely suspended. [Unemployed workingmen] *have no means to get away from the pest-ridden cities; for*

Left: Grave of Armstrong Flowers. *Ryan Starrett.*

Right: The church at Rocky Springs. *Ryan Starrett.*

Plaque at the town of Rocky Springs, milepost 54.8. *Ryan Starrett.*

them there is no labor, no wages, no bread—nothing but death or starvation, and this condition must last at least for fifty days, for there will be no stay of the pestilence, no resumption of business until frost.[41]

Armstrong Ellis Flowers served his state in the Thirty-Eighth Mississippi Regiment. He survived Billy Yank's bullets and all the concomitant diseases that accompanied an army during wartime, but he could not survive Yellow Jack. He succumbed to the fever during the pandemic of 1878. He was fifty-five years old.

Rocky Springs was a town of 2,600 people—127 caught the fever that year; 51 of them never recovered and joined Flowers in death. Just five years before, pastor J.W. Sandwell reported 180 cases and 43 deaths in Rocky Springs. Between the Civil War, yellow fever and, later, the boll weevil, the town ceased to exist.[42]

TEN-YEAR-OLD FLORENCE IRENE WAS terrified of storms. Whenever the thunder and lightning began, she would run to her mother for comfort. Her mother, Ellen Ford, was only too happy to provide it, for her daughter was "as bright and affectionate a Daughter as ever God with His Image blest." In

Tomb of Florence Irene Ford, Natchez City Cemetery. *Ryan Starrett.*

1871, though, there was only so much comfort Ellen could give her beloved daughter. Unlike storms, which pass, yellow fever all too often was the end of the road. Ellen gave what comfort she could, but she could not protect her daughter from the sickness that killed so many of that era.

Distraught at her inability to protect her daughter, Ellen and her husband, Washington, buried Florence in a casket with a window at her head. They also built a six-foot staircase leading into the tomb. Whenever it stormed, Ellen would descend the stairs to be with her daughter. She would shut the trapdoors at the head of the stairs, take a seat next to Florence and read or sing to her until the storm passed.

Cypress Swamps at milepost 122 of the Natchez Trace. *Ryan Starrett.*

Not long after, Washington and Ellen Ford left Natchez for good. To ensure that Florence would always have a guardian, her parents left behind a stone angel sitting atop her tomb. For the last century and a half, it has stood guard, storm or shine.[43]

Chapter 4

BLEEDING COUNTRY

FRIENDS AND ENEMIES ON THE CUMBERLAND RIVER

THE AMBUSH

For sixty-five years, the image had haunted William Hall: two tomahawks, striking his brother's temple simultaneously. On a hot wilderness road in 1787, just northeast of the new settlement of Nashville, Hall had watched his brother fall and die.

Hall and his family had been living at their homestead near the Cumberland River for two years. They were some of the first white people to move into that wild land. His father built their house, while Hall and his mother and siblings waited in nearby Bledsoe's Fort.

Any settler on the western frontier knew that Indians were dangerous. Indian raiders had harassed the Cumberland settlements from the beginning, stealing horses and killing settlers. So many settlers fell in the first years that, as one early historian put it, "death seemed ready to embrace the whole of the adventurers." A fort like Bledsoe's, with high timber walls, was a necessary precursor to settlement.[44]

Hall's father moved his family out of the fort and into their home in the winter of 1785. It didn't take long for raiders to notice them. The following spring, the Hall family's horses—twelve or fifteen of them—disappeared, led away to an Indian town. The family was so shaken by the theft that they left their homestead and moved back into the fort for several months. But as frontier families so often did, they decided to return to their settlement and hope—and fight—for the best.

A painting of Fort Nashborough, which protected the earliest Cumberland River settlers. *Wikimedia Commons.*

The land that the Halls and their peers were willing to risk their lives for was a new Eden beyond the Appalachian Mountains. The settlers must have been enticed by early descriptions of the land that made it sound like paradise. Hundred-pound catfish swam in the Cumberland, and bear, elk, deer and bison abounded. Crops yielded double what they did on the other side of the mountains. A 1793 tract summarized the land: "Few places are more healthy; there is none more fertile; and there is hardly any other place, in which the farmer can support his family in such a degree of affluence." The tract did not mention frequent Indian raids.[45]

The Indians most hostile to the presence of settlers along the Cumberland River were a faction of Cherokee led by a chief named Dragging Canoe. Dragging Canoe rejected the legitimacy of settler claims in Middle Tennessee, breaking with the larger Cherokee Nation. He resolved to drive the settlers out.

Deeply concerned by the Indian raids, James Robertson, a founder of the Nashville settlement, organized a large company of volunteer militia to march to the Cherokee towns and demand that they send a delegation for peace talks. The march was meant to be a show of force that stopped short of actual violence. Dragging Canoe complied, sending his brother Little Owl to Nashville to discuss peace. William Hall's father, a magistrate of newly formed Sumner County, was invited to attend the peace talks. He left for Nashville.

Unbeknownst to him, Little Owl's visit was a ruse. While the elder Hall treated with Little Owl, fifteen Cherokee warriors took positions on the road outside Hall's house. Thirteen-year-old William Hall and his brother James were the first unfortunate people to travel along the road that day, past ten Cherokee warriors hidden behind a pile of logs. Ahead, five more warriors hid in the boughs of a tree, ready to open fire with their rifles or drop down and attack with tomahawks. Hall and his brother were oblivious to their presence.

As the brothers walked along the road, they discussed the task they had been given by their father: how best to retrieve their horses from their neighbor's pasture, about a quarter mile from their house. William thought they should lure the horses with corn. He turned around to get his brother's opinion on the subject, just in time to see ten warriors silently surrounding

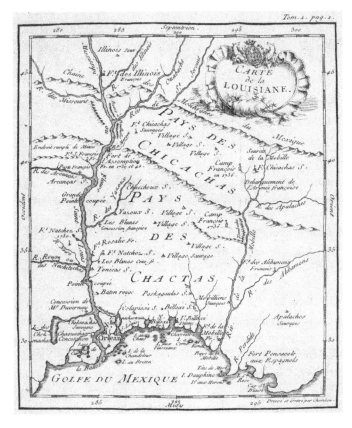

A map of the Southeast published in *Mémoires Historiques sur la Louisiane* in 1753. *Internet Archive.*

them. James Hall, alerted by his brother's look of shock, turned around, and then the tomahawks fell on his head.

In that moment, William Hall had a decision to make. He could fight, which would be suicidal. He could surrender, which would likely also be suicidal. Or he could run. He decided to run.

The five Cherokee hiding in the tree ahead dropped from their position and tried to catch the boy. They got to within feet of him, swinging their tomahawks. But the fleet Hall managed to scramble away, into the canebrake beside the road. Hall was slim, athletic and unencumbered by weapons. Each of the Cherokee carried a rifle and a hatchet. In the canebrake, Hall proved too fast and nimble to be caught. He ran the quarter mile back to his house, the Cherokee pursuing him the whole way. Fortunately for Hall, a group of six armed neighborhood men had just arrived at his house. The Indians turned and fled.

Hall led the six neighbors back to where his brother James lay. He had been scalped. Soon word reached militiamen at Fort Bledsoe, and a small group set out in pursuit of the Cherokee. They caught up with the Indians and wounded two, but ultimately they escaped, leaving behind a bloody tomahawk and a backpack onto which was tied James Hall's scalp.[46]

RETALIATION

James Robertson was an archetypal frontiersman who seemed drawn to the harshest living conditions by nature. When he arrived at the Cumberland River in 1779 to plant corn and establish a settlement in Middle Tennessee, the land was so removed from civilization that Americans did not know much about it. The American colonies claimed the land, but Robertson and his benefactor, Richard Henderson, who had first hatched the idea of a settlement on the Cumberland, could not even agree on whether the land fell within the jurisdiction of Virginia or North Carolina.

For them, the proper course of action was to settle the land and then work out details of ownership later. Of course, they hoped and trusted that many thousands of acres would soon come into their own respective possessions.

The land they claimed had not been unoccupied before Robertson arrived. One of the earliest written descriptions of the settlements along the Cumberland, from 1793, notes that the Indians who had formerly inhabited the area must have been numerous—there were burial sites and the remains of towns every five or six miles along the river. More Indians seemed to have

Painting of James Robertson by Washington B. Cooper. *Internet Archive.*

lived along the Cumberland than almost anywhere else.[47]

On a map of North America published in London in 1776, Middle Tennessee is mostly featureless, with labels suggesting the contested ownership of the area; the word *Cherakees* is written in large letters across the area, but *Nth Carolina* is written in even larger letters. The Cherokee claimed the land and even sold to Henderson's Transylvania Company a 20-million-acre portion of it comprising the majority of present-day Kentucky and parts of surrounding states, in exchange for "a cabin full of trade goods." The deal was later nullified by Virginia, which still allotted 200,000 acres to the company. Henderson eventually looked south to land on the Cumberland and planned his settlement there.[48]

Dragging Canoe objected to the 20-million-acre sale but could not stop it. He would soon decide that if he could not stop white settlement by treaty, he would stop it by bloodshed.

The settlers along the Cumberland River in those days could only look to the vast wilderness that surrounded them and speculate about where hostile Indians lived, from which villages they attacked and to which villages they retreated. Settlers knew the locations of some villages but were not even aware that others existed.

So it was in 1787. The Cumberland settlers found themselves living in a "bleeding country," as Robertson put it in a letter. They were dejected, fearful and subject to daily raids that originated from they knew not whence. They suspected that the raids came from Running Water and Nickajack, Cherokee towns located on the Tennessee River roughly one hundred miles southeast of Nashville. The towns were highly defensible, with mountains to the east, river to the north and west and Creek allies and wilderness to the south. From the towns, Dragging Canoe controlled traffic on the Tennessee River.[49]

But the Cumberland settlers were looking in the wrong direction. In reality, the Cherokee raids were originating from another town along the Tennessee River, much farther to the west at Muscle Shoals. The settlement was called Coldwater Town, and the Cherokee raiders appreciated that the

Photo of the Tennessee River from 1926. *Library of Congress.*

location afforded them easy access to the Cumberland settlements via a direct overland route: the Natchez Trace.[50]

But the Trace ran through the domain of another tribe, the Chickasaw. And they would prove to be the key to stopping the raids. The Chickasaw, longtime allies of the British before the American Revolution, found themselves courted by Spain and the United States in the 1780s. In 1786, the Chickasaw, led by Piomingo, signed a peace treaty with the United States at Hopewell, South Carolina. Piomingo surmised that the United States was a superior military power whose expansion could not be stopped. By signing the treaty at Hopewell, he hoped to maximize the Chickasaw's trading opportunities, increase their own military power and allow them to remain

44

independent of the far more populous Creek Nation, which was hostile to white settlement in Tennessee and set on war.[51]

The treaty put the Chickasaw under the protection of the United States, set clear boundaries for the Chickasaw Nation, established rights of travel for traders and forbade murder and theft by Americans of Chickasaw and vice versa. Crucially, the treaty required that the Chickasaw inform the government of the United States if they discovered any plotting by Indians of other nations.[52]

The treaty was soon tested when two Chickasaw hunters traveling along the Tennessee River discovered Coldwater Town in 1787. The Indians there welcomed them to spend the night and shared stories of their raids on the Cumberland settlements. The Chickasaw must have also noticed the presence of French traders at Coldwater Town, as well as the fact that the traders had been supplying the Indians there with rifles. The two hunters returned to their nation and told their chief, Piomingo, what they had discovered. Piomingo sent the hunters to Nashville to report the location of Coldwater Town. His decision to inform the Americans was fortuitous and would prove the foundation of a strong alliance.

Robertson, who had been lobbying Governor Richard Caswell of North Carolina for help, was moved to action on June 13, 1787, when a raid near his own home killed his brother. Having just learned of the existence of Coldwater Town, Robertson organized a punitive force of 130 volunteers and departed immediately, following the southbound trail the killers of his brother had left in the dense undergrowth. Piomingo's two Chickasaw messengers would help guide the expedition.

Robertson and his force split up, with Captain David Hay taking fifty men to the mouth of Duck River, downriver from Coldwater Town. He would intercept any fleeing Cherokee or French traders. Robertson took the remainder of the volunteers overland, via a circuitous route that followed the Natchez Trace and several creeks and ended at the Tennessee River near the southern end of Muscle Shoals. There, a few Cherokee warriors detected Robertson's men and skirmished with them before fleeing. The element of surprise had been lost.

ROBERTSON'S MEN CAMPED FOR a few hours and at nightfall began crossing the Tennessee River using a leaky forty-man Indian canoe. On the other side lay a village that had been alerted and abandoned a few hours before. From the village, a westward path disappeared into the forest. They rested and prepared to head west to Coldwater Town.

Charactcrıshch Chicasaw head

An early depiction of a Chickasaw man, published in 1776, before the Cumberland settlers arrived in Middle Tennessee. *Beinecke Library at Yale University.*

Robertson and his men walked and rode along the path for eighteen miles. By the time they reached Coldwater Creek and the village just beyond, the warriors of Coldwater Town had known of their presence for three days. But somehow, Robertson's men were able to reach the creek without alerting the warriors. Some of Robertson's men took positions on the east side of the creek, and some crossed to the west side in single file, where the cabins of Coldwater Town lay. After they had crossed, they erupted into a full-scale attack on the town.

The startled residents fled in all directions. Some ran toward Coldwater Creek, where a group of Robertson's men lay in ambush. Many headed north to the Tennessee River, where they boarded canoes and tried to paddle away. Robertson's men fired from the bank of the river, puncturing the canoes and their passengers with lead. Some abandoned their boats, jumping in the river in hopes of swimming to safety. As many as twenty-six people died in the river, including three French men and a French woman. Accounts of the attack do not say how many Indian women and children were killed.

The majority of the dead were Cherokee, but six Creek, including a chief, had also been killed—a fact that would have dire consequences for young William Hall and his family. Six French traders surrendered and were taken prisoner, along with an Indian woman and child.

Robertson's men filled four canoes with captured rum, sugar, coffee, clothes, blankets, salt, shot, knives, powder, tomahawks and tobacco. They rewarded their Chickasaw guides with a horse and rifle each, ammunition and as many blankets and as much clothing as they could carry. Robertson killed the livestock around the village and put Coldwater Town to the torch. He had dealt a decisive and merciless blow to his enemies.

Robertson and his men headed for the river crossing that would come to be known as Colbert's Crossing, crossed back to the north side of the Tennessee River and headed for the Natchez Trace to return to Nashville. In all, the expedition took nineteen days.[53]

Colbert's Stand, milepost 327.3. *Ryan Starrett.*

Site of George Colbert's Stand. *Ryan Starrett.*

THE CYCLE OF REVENGE

In the wake of James Hall's murder, the Hall family once again faced a choice: stick it out at their homestead or retreat to the safety of Bledsoe's Fort. James Hall was killed in early June, and a retreat to the fort would mean the family would be abandoning its farm during the growing season. The historical record does not contain details of the anguished debating the Hall family must have undergone while still grieving the murder of a son. Ultimately, the family convened with the leaders of the two other households in the area, and together they decided to stay on their farms for the summer. But to prevent another Indian attack, they would hire two young men to guard the three farms.

In the weeks following James Hall's murder, James Robertson and his volunteers wiped Coldwater Town off the map—only a few days after being marked on the map. But in doing so, the men had killed six Creek men from villages scattered throughout the Creek Nation. Although Creek warriors had participated in Cherokee raids on the Cumberland settlements before, they now had cause to launch their own revenge-driven raids against the settlements.

For two months, all was quiet. Then, in early August, the guards arrived at the Hall family homestead with a message: *Get to the fort immediately. The Creek are coming, and there are a lot of them.* The Hall family began frantically packing a sled. They would not just seek refuge in the fort—they would

Creek Chief Se-Loc-Ta. *Library of Congress.*

move to the fort for the foreseeable future. They set off, some driving horses and some on foot. Another of William Hall's brothers and a neighbor accompanied the sled as guards. About a half mile from the house, while crossing a stream, the horses spooked. William Hall, who must have been especially rattled after his near murder two months before, suspected Indians were near. But his older brother urged them on. They made it to the fort safely.

Although the group had made it to the fort, the elder Hall gambled that he could return to his homestead for another load of possessions. His calculus would prove to be dead wrong. The Halls had made two more trips back and forth to their homestead. Three successful trips must have comforted the elder Hall. He decided to go back for a fourth—and final—time.

The day was nearly over. The Halls reached their homestead, loaded the sled once more and set off toward Bledsoe's Fort. Two guards—one of them William's older brother Richard—walked at the head of the group, weapons ready. William Hall came next, mounted and pulling the sled. Behind him rode William's younger brother John and younger sister Prudence. William Hall's father, mother and a brother-in-law followed behind.

The group approached a fallen ash tree whose top was lying across the road. They must have passed the fallen tree several times already that day. But this time, a small dog traveling with them began barking furiously as they approached. Richard Hall walked slowly toward the treetop. William Hall spotted something: a rifle barrel sticking through the leaves. He must have noticed it at the same moment the rifle's hammer struck down. Richard Hall was struck twice in the body.

At the report of the rifles, the rest of the Creek party—forty or fifty warriors—emerged from their hiding places, "yelling like demons," William Hall would later remember, and charged toward the remaining Hall siblings. The other guard who had accompanied them, a man named Hickerson, stood his ground in the middle of the road, aiming his rifle and firing at the approaching Indians. His rifle misfired. It likely would have made no difference. In a moment, his body was riddled with six or seven shots. Richard Hall stumbled into the woods but soon fell dead.

William Hall dismounted and grabbed his two younger siblings, running back toward his mother and father. William Hall's father made a stand with his son-in-law, advancing and firing toward the Indians while the children scrambled into the woods. The son-in-law felt bullets piercing his body and made for the woods. William Hall's father continued his stand, one against dozens.

The horses that had been pulling the Hall family sled bolted when the gunfire erupted, overturning and splintering the sled. The Hall family's possessions scattered across the road.

William Hall's mother had been riding a horse that had also spooked at the sound of the gunfire. With no control over the animal, Hall's mother rode toward the fort, directly into the party of Indians. Somehow she made it through without injury.

From the shelter of the woods, William Hall listened for the report of his father's heavy rifle. He heard the distinctive crack among many other shots.

He heard the Indians whoop. He did not hear his father's rifle any longer. Later, they would find the man lying by the side of the road, scalped and shot thirteen times. The Indian raiders had taken his rifle and fled immediately.

William Hall, thinking that his two younger siblings stood a better chance of survival at their homestead, sent them back alone. They made it but, frightened by dogs, turned and started again for the fort. Alone, they walked the whole way there, picking up a hat and a pail of butter among the wreckage of their sled. No harm came to them as they walked alone at night on the road.

William Hall made for the fort—someone had to tell the others what had happened. For all he knew, he was the only one to survive the attack. When men from the fort rode out to the scene, they found not only William Hall's father and brother lying dead but also his brother-in-law—somehow he had survived several gunshot wounds and would go on to recover.

In the aftermath of the ambush, William Hall took stock. His mother and two younger siblings had survived, but his father and two of his brothers had fallen. The family, who had felt so hopeful a few months before, were shattered. The Cherokee and Creek resistance to white settlement had succeeded in driving one frontier family from their homestead. But ultimately, the settler tide would prove inexorable.[54]

HARD-EARNED PEACE

After the attack on Coldwater Town, a confederacy of the Creek and Cherokee Nations, with the help of a tribe of Delaware, turned their attention to the Chickasaw. Outraged at their alliance with the Cumberland settlers, they sent war parties to harass the Chickasaw in their own nation and along the Trace.

Piomingo, the Chickasaw chief who had signed the treaty with the United States at Hopewell and had been instrumental in facilitating the successful attack at Coldwater Town, vowed to keep the Natchez Trace clear of marauding Creek and Cherokee. But being greatly outnumbered by the larger nations, he could not stop attacks. Nearly every white traveler from the Cumberland settlements was attacked by hostile Indians en route to the Chickasaw towns. Even a decade later, the Englishman Francis Baily was deathly afraid of Creek raiders while traveling the Natchez Trace from Natchez to Nashville.

The Creek confederacy took special umbrage at Piomingo's cooperation and vowed to assassinate him. They did not succeed, but they did kill two of his close relatives. Eventually, the depredations on the Chickasaw led to war between the Chickasaw and Creek.

The hostilities deepened the relationship between the Cumberland settlers and the Chickasaw. They became comrades in a mutual conflict. The Cumberland settlers sent volunteers to help defend the Chickasaw homeland. President George Washington, eager to please the Chickasaw, sent them long rifles, three thousand pounds of ammunition and fearsome "swivel guns"—small mounted cannons that James Robertson himself showed the Chickasaw how to use. Thousands more pounds of lead and gunpowder, hundreds of rifles, flints, beef, corn and whiskey flowed south to the Chickasaw. The support in materiel made Piomingo the most powerful chief in the Southeast.

Eventually, the Creek realized that a war on the Chickasaw meant they would have to contend with the Cumberland settlements and the United States, and they made peace. The Chickasaw came to be regarded as heroes in Nashville—the friends who offered aid to a people beset by enemies.

William Hall, who survived two Cherokee ambushes in his teenage years, grew up to become governor of Tennessee. Militiamen from Tennessee and Kentucky dealt the Cherokee another decisive military defeat at the towns of Nickajack and Running Water in 1794, effectively ending the Cherokee threat to the Cumberland settlements and paving the way for Cherokee dispossession in the East.[55]

Chapter 5

THE DUELISTS

NORRIS WRIGHT, SAMUEL GWIN AND HENRY VICK

Major Norris Wright:
The Man Who Woke a Sleeping Tiger

Rapides Parish, Louisiana, 1824

The forged ballots had been a success. Major Norris Wright had defeated his opponent, Samuel Wells, for the position of sheriff of Rapides Parish by a handful of votes.

Alexandria, Louisiana, December 14, 1826

James Bowie sailed into Alexandria from Arkansas, where he had been attempting to amass more land through fraudulent speculation. His brother and friends greeted him at the dock and told him all that Norris Wright had said about his questionable land dealings in his absence. Armed only with a small pistol and a clasp knife, Bowie stormed over to Bailey's Hotel.

Major Wright was inside entertaining friends. When an angry Bowie demanded an explanation, Wright drew his pistol and pointed it at the man's chest. Bowie countered with a chair, and when he raised it to smash Wright on the head, Wright fired at point-blank range. It was nearly a fateful mistake, for Bowie leaped on him and began pounding his face. Pinning him to the ground, Bowie withdrew a clasp knife, and as he was opening it to

Norris Wright hovering above a fallen Jim Bowie just before the former's death, as seen at the Natchez Visitor Center. *Ryan Starrett.*

finish Wright off, the latter's friends intervened and pulled Bowie off—but not before he left a tooth in Wright's hand. Then Bowie's friends intervened and carried him upstairs. Preferring to finish off the wounded man, Wright gathered some comrades and began to pursue Bowie, but upon seeing so much blood on the stairs, Wright's company assumed the wound was mortal and left the hotel as a group.[56]

Rapides Parish, January 1827

"I have seen some faces in town as long as Don Quixote's," remarked Judge Henry Bullard when he saw Norris Wright, recently defeated sheriff, walking through town. Wright was furious that he had been defeated in his reelection campaign, but he had simply made too many enemies. On this day, he pledged eternal enmity toward his successful opponent, Samuel Wells, and Wells's close friends Robert Crain and James Bowie.

Wright had his own friends. In the interconnected world of east Louisiana and west Mississippi, filled with machismo and guns, it was necessary to have as many friends as possible. More importantly, it was necessary to have the right kind of friends—friends who knew how and weren't afraid to use a pistol.

Natchez, September 18, 1827

Samuel Wells arrived in Natchez from across the river. He met with his old friend, Dr. Thomas Maddox, and the two agreed to settle their recent differences on the field of honor in the Mississippi River. Their dispute would be settled on an island because the two states bordering it had recently cracked down on dueling.

Norris Wright agreed that he would go to support his friend Thomas Maddox. But he was worried that other, less reputable characters from Louisiana might arrive—one of whom, James Bowie, he was in no mood to cross paths with. Wells and Maddox agreed that while spectators could come, only the duelists, their seconds and their doctors would take the field. Assured that Bowie would not arrive, Wright committed to going as a distant supporter and witness.

He would bring along pistols and a shotgun, though, just in case.

Natchez, September 19, 1827

> *A number of persons of respectable standing (12 or 15 in number) arrived in this city and vicinity, on Sunday and Monday last, from Alexandria, La. With the avowed purpose...of settling some personal difficulties, by private combat. The vicinity of this city, on the margin of the Mississippi, it appears, was selected by them for their battleground.*[57]
> —*Natchez Weekly Democrat*

A sandbar between Natchez and Vidalia, September 19, 1827

Wright and a few friends stayed about four hundred yards behind as the two duelists met at the agreed-on location. Following the Code Duello, Wells and Maddox fired two shots apiece. Satisfied that honor had been fulfilled, they decided the matter had been settled and they would have a glass of wine. The six decided to join the party of Maddox, where Wright awaited them. As they headed that way, Bowie's party came toward them at a "run-walk." Robert Crain, Maddox's second, saw several armed men—including General Samuel Cuny, a Wells supporter and avowed enemy—and drew his pistol. It was one

"Snakes in a Saw Pit" from 1791. *Beinecke Library at Yale University.*

against a handful. Cuny and Bowie drew theirs. Crain and Bowie exchanged futile shots. Crain fired his second pistol quickly and hit Cuny in the thigh, severing his artery, and then, defenseless, he took off in the direction of his friends. Bowie pursued, knife in hand. Just before Bowie caught him, Crain turned around and hurled his pistol, knocking Bowie to the ground.

Just at that moment, Wright and another spectator came rushing to the aid of their friend Crain. Bowie yelled from behind a five-foot tree, "Wright, you damned rascal, don't you shoot me!" Bowie's friend tossed him a pistol, and the two fired almost simultaneously, both missing. But Wright had another gun; Bowie did not.

"Shoot and be damned," Bowie cried, thinking they'd be his last words. They should have been, but then George McWhorter, Bowie's friend, fired a bullet into Wright's left side. Believing his own wound to be mortal, Wright approached Bowie and fired into the right side of his chest—just as he had done at Bailey's Hotel nine months ago.

And then, just like nine months ago, Bowie refused to go down. Instead, he began to chase Wright, who took off running. Fortunately for the latter, two of his friends arrived and fired at the wounded tiger, hitting him in the thigh. With Bowie now grounded, Wright whipped around and drew his sword cane. So did his partner. It was two swords against a knife and free hand. Only it was Bowie's knife.

That knife ended up in Wright's chest as Bowie whispered in his ear, "Now, Major, you die!" Norris Wright collapsed and died in the arms of the man he loathed and feared. The melee ended when Bowie's last assailant was shot in the arm and stabbed by Bowie himself, who had finally managed to escape from underneath Wright's body.

Dr. William Provan of Natchez emerged from the safety of the woods. He immediately approached the prone Wright and opened his vest. Bowie had twisted the knife once he plunged it into Wright's chest. Prozan's prognosis was an easy one.

In the end, General Cluny and Major Wright lost their lives on that sandbar in the Mississippi River. Several others were wounded. And one legend was born. The price? Two more graves along the Father of Waters.[58]

SAMUEL GWIN: A CATCALL GONE TOO FAR

January 30, 1835

Andrew Jackson stared at the pistol, ten feet away and pointed at his chest. The cap exploded but failed to light the powder. The angry president charged his assailant, only to see the man raise a second pistol and fire. It, too, failed to ignite the powder.[59]

The would-be assassin, Richard Lawrence, then fled from the House chamber, with Jackson in hot pursuit. Lawrence was quickly taken down and apprehended. A shaken Jackson blamed the assassination attempt on a disgruntled Whig Party. Specifically, he blamed Senator George Poindexter of Clinton, Mississippi.[60]

SAMUEL GWIN WAS FURIOUS when he heard the news regarding an assassination attempt on the president, his friend. Gwin's father, Methodist minister James Gwin, had been a stalwart supporter and friend of the president as long as Samuel could remember. Samuel himself had fought with Old Hickory during his campaign against the Creeks, at the Battle of Horseshoe Bend, during the siege of Pensacola in 1814 and at the Battle of New Orleans,

Andrew Jackson as president. *Library of Congress.*

in which the sons of the Revolution proved their mettle to their fathers. The elder Gwin fought and ministered to Jackson's troops, earning him everlasting gratitude from the most powerful man in the country.[61]

Reverend James Gwin's son Samuel reaped the benefits of his and his father's loyalty when Jackson appointed him register of the land office at Mount Salus, Mississippi. The nomination defined the "spoils system."[62] Nevertheless, Samuel was exceedingly grateful. He explained why in a letter to Mississippi senator George Poindexter:

> [I] *was a volunteer under Jackson in his Indian campaigns; was in Coffee's brigade in the assault and capture of Pensacola in 1814, and in all the engagements with the British below New Orleans. I lost my health by long protracted exposure, and to this day am a habitual suffer[er]. In 1829 the Postmaster General was good enough to give me a clerkship in his department, since which time I have never been absent from my post. My beloved wife is now threatened with consumption, and I am advised that the only hope for her is to take her to a warmer climate. Under this advice, and with this hope, and for the happiness of a young family, I submitted the case to the President, and, with the noble sympathies of his nature, he conferred on me the Mount Salus appointment.*[63]

Poindexter was not impressed. He did not want a non-Mississippian to occupy a federal post in Mississippi.[64] He fought to reject Samuel's appointment and won. Four years later, Samuel—and his brother, William—campaigned against Poindexter as he sought reelection as a Whig to the U.S. Senate. Poindexter's opponent, Robert Walker, won in a tight race.

January 1836

Whig Charles Lynch was inaugurated governor of Mississippi. An inaugural dinner was held, and the transition was going smoothly. The dinner was a success, and then Poindexter, loaded with alcohol, stood atop a table and damned President Andrew Jackson and his Democratic Party. As the harangue continued, Samuel Gwin began to boo and "hiss." Others joined in. Isaac Caldwell, a former Mississippi Supreme Court judge and law partner of Poindexter, arose in a fury and made his way to Gwin. In a patriotic display of Whigish support and Mississippi pride, he issued a duel to the Tennessee-born Gwin. The challenge was promptly accepted. In public. At a gubernatorial election party.

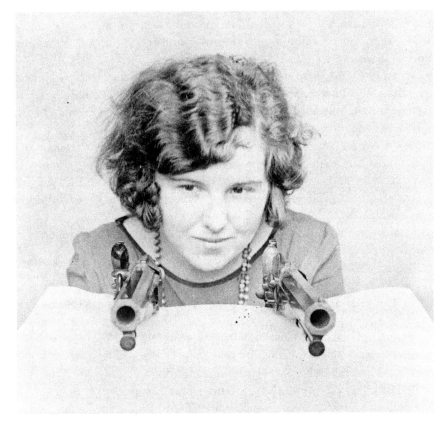

Grace Stockman poses behind Andrew Jackson's dueling pistols. *Library of Congress.*

MOST DUELS—CALDWELL HAD BEEN involved in at least one before, possibly two—were settled in secrecy.[65] The Code Duello was a set ritual involving seconds, surgeons, negotiations and, more often than not, shots being fired into the air to satisfy honor. Far more duels were "fought" and settled than ended in fatalities. After all, Mississippi had instituted anti-dueling laws since 1799. These early laws were expanded and became popularly known, ironically, as the "Poindexter Code of 1822."[66] To kill someone in a duel could potentially end in a murder charge. However, the Caldwell-Gwin challenge had been issued and accepted before too many people.

On the morning of January 12, four to five hundred people showed up at Raymond Road, about a mile from town, to witness Gwin and Caldwell take shots at each other (or to have it settled by the seconds or to watch pistols fired into the air and then a handshake but also, just possibly, to witness a de facto and de jure murder). Among the spectators were the mayor of Clinton, city aldermen and reporters from Vicksburg and Jackson.

When Gwin accepted the challenge, he agreed to a duel with two braces of pistols, meaning each duelist would receive four total shots[67] at thirty paces. The duel would be conducted in the Russian style—meaning each duelist would advance on his opponent, firing at will.[68]

At the signal, Gwin began advancing. Caldwell fired and fired again and again and again. One of his four shots struck Gwin in his chest. But Gwin, too, was firing and continued to do so. His third shot finally struck Caldwell in the abdomen. The latter immediately crumpled to the ground. Within two hours, Isaac Caldwell was dead.[69]

Samuel Gwin survived two more years but never fully recovered. He finally succumbed to his injuries in New Orleans on July 25, 1838.

HENRY VICK : A WEDDING BECOMES A FUNERAL

It was one of the best days of Helen Johnstone's young life. She and her mother sauntered down Canal Street in New Orleans. They had made the two-hundred-mile trek from their home in Madison County, Mississippi, in search of the perfect dress. It had to be perfect because it was destined for her perfect day—the day she would marry Henry Vick at the Chapel of the Cross in her hometown.

Helen and her mom found a beautiful bridal trousseau, enjoyed an exotic meal in New Orleans[70] and excitedly hurried home to prepare for the big day.

A DIRECT DESCENDANT OF Newitt Vick, founder of Vicksburg, Henry Vick had made a good match for himself. His bride-to-be was the daughter of John and Margaret Johnstone, the owners of Annandale Plantation. When the patriarch died in 1848, his wife built the Chapel of the Cross to honor his memory. Upon completion in 1852, she transferred the church and its surrounding ten acres to the Episcopal Diocese of Mississippi. It was in this church that he was to marry Helen.[71]

But first he, too, made a pre-wedding trip to New Orleans. He planned to pick up his wedding suit and shop for household items requested by his bride-to-be. He stopped at Annandale and picked up the list from Helen,

Gravestone of Henry Vick at the Chapel of the Cross in Madison, Mississippi. *Ryan Starrett.*

kissed her goodbye and headed to New Orleans. His odyssey, though, involved a stop at a pool hall. It did not end with a leisurely stroll through the Crescent City but rather a measured walk through a killing field in Mobile, Alabama.

THE *NEW ORLEANS CRESCENT* reported on the duel near Mobile between Henry Vick and James Stith:

> *The parties, we learned, did not leave Vicksburg to fight, but had a sudden difficulty in this city, which led to the meeting at Mobile. As we hear it, they came together in a billiard-room in this city, where a gentleman who was friendly to both offered to introduce them, not supposing that they knew each other, and not being able to construe their distantness into their mutual remembrance of an old college difficulty. Mr. Vick declined the introduction, flatly: the gentleman who had offered the introduction stepped aside with him, to ask him the reason of his refusal: he said that he would not recognize Mr. Stith as a gentleman: Mr. Stith, overhearing this, approached Mr. Vick and struck him: then followed the challenge from Mr. Vick, the trip to Mobile, and the fatal result. Mr. Vick was the only son of Col. Henry Vick of Issaquena County, Mississippi: and Mr. Stith also belongs to one of the oldest families of that State.[72]*

Vick's body was placed on a ship headed north toward Vicksburg. Unbeknownst to them, the caterers for the wedding were on the same boat.[73] Meanwhile, back in Madison, at the Chapel of the Cross, Helen was arranging flowers for her wedding day. Henry, like his fiancée Helen, returned home. Unlike Helen, the local papers followed the bridegroom's return to Mississippi with avid interest:

> *Mr. Vick's remains passed through this place Sunday evening, accompanied by twelve young men of Vicksburg as pallbearers, and immediate relatives and friends, including the lovely young lady to whom he was betrothed. It was a sad spectacle—sad to think that one so noble as he reputedly was—that just as he had actively entered upon life's arena with aspirations high, and heart of generous throb—should thus be sacrificed on that altar which a false and deplorable state of public sentiment has griped with the name of "honor."[74]*

Helen, with her beautiful dress and veil and her high hopes for the future, as well as her entombed love recently placed at her feet, pleaded with her mother to bury Henry at the Chapel of the Cross. Her distraught mother acquiesced. Instead of the wedding he planned to preside over in the morning, Bishop William Mercer Green performed the Burial of the Dead that very evening, with the bride alongside the coffin that held her betrothed.[75]

Chapter 6

THE SAUCE OF HUNGER

SCROUNGING FOR FOOD ON THE TRACE

The Preacher

His work in the Mississippi Territory was done for the moment. And what a magnificent climax his preaching had reached at that campsite in the wilderness. For four days, Lorenzo Dow had ministered to the settlers along the Trace north of Natchez. The last time he visited, the area was the domain of "scape-gallows" and heathens, but now he could see God converting the countryside.

Dow had awakened fifty souls at his December camp meeting. Five had publicly professed their faith. Dow, with his long, dark hair and big, piercing eyes, had moved people. It wasn't uncommon for backsliders to drop to their knees and weep at his services. He could bring a crowd to ecstatic silence or set worshipers to "jerking"—moving their bodies uncontrollably to a celestial rhythm. Dow and his flock had produced so much noise at their campsite that critics had stopped by to taunt him. "Is God deaf?" one asked.

The devil's emissaries, Dow thought. *We beat the devil this time.*

Now Dow would return north. He would take the Trace, as he had done before. He secured three half-wild Spanish horses, packed provisions and set off with two companions. For five days, the riding went smoothly, although two of the horses had spooked, bucking and rearing wildly. On the sixth day, they came to the Pearl River and were faced with one of the most harrowing parts of a Natchez Trace journey: fording a waterway that could grow or shrink wildly depending on the weather and season.

Lorenzo Dow. *Library of Congress.*

The Pearl had shrunk considerably since Dow had crossed it a few weeks before. It was only five or six feet wide. *This shouldn't be a problem*, he thought. He and his companions set about leading their horses across. Dow didn't realize when he stepped into the cold water that the channel, although narrow, was swift and powerful. Dow's mare made it to the opposite bank, but when she stepped on the soil, it gave way. Dow and his mare were swept into the muddy current. Dow could not swim, and at that moment he thought he might drown. But his strong Spanish mare managed to swim back to shore and scramble her way up the bank, extracting a wet, chilled and frightened Dow.

He had made it across the Pearl, but the mishap had created a new dilemma. When Dow's mare had her footing, his coffee, sugar, tea and other provisions had been washed into the river, never to be recovered. Now Dow and his companions would have to ride through the wilderness with insufficient food. And there were few places along the Trace to resupply.

The three rode on. Dow grew feverish. Their supplies ran out completely. It took four days to reach Silas Dinsmoor's agency house, north of the Choctaw villages. Dinsmoor didn't have much to share, but as always, Dow managed to resupply and continue his journey—after doing a little more preaching of course.

Dow's ordeal at the Pearl River highlights a persistent problem facing travelers along the early Trace: how to feed oneself during a long and arduous journey through the wilderness. To solve the problem, travelers took a multi-pronged approach. They invariably carried provisions with them. They relied on the abundant wild food present along the Trace. They ate the domesticated plants of the Choctaw and Chickasaw. And eventually, they came to depend on the "houses of entertainment" that entrepreneurs opened on the road for the purpose of accommodating travelers.[76]

PROVISIONS

No one knew better how to provision a journey than John Blommart. He had served as a sailor in the Royal Navy for eighteen years, subsisting on the foods that could be stowed away in a ship's hold for weeks at a time: biscuits, beef and pork casked in salt; peas; rice; raisins; olive oil; oatmeal; butter; and cheese, as well as, of course, beer, wine and rum. After his service as a sailor, he had been agent victualler at Pensacola, arranging for those same foods to be supplied to Royal Navy ships leaving his port.

When he became one of the first British men to open a store at the river landing in Natchez, he made sure his store was stocked with items that would keep on a long journey: hams, bacon, smoked beef, sugar and liquor. He might have sold "ship's biscuits," simple unleavened discs made from flour, water and salt.

Blommart would have mostly provisioned river travelers at his store at the landing—foot traffic up the Natchez Trace was still sparse. But within a few decades, traders from upriver would begin traveling the Trace by the thousand. And they would need to carry their food on their backs or in their horses' saddlebags.[77]

When the Englishman Francis Baily and twelve companions planned a trip up the Trace in 1797, they made sure to load their horses with the

"Man with a Slaughtered Pig," by Giuseppe Maria Matelli. *Rijksmuseum.*

food they would need along the way. They had an ox killed and the meat dried. They had twenty-five pounds of "ship's biscuit" baked by a Spanish soldier who knew the esoteric recipe. They packed six pounds of flour, twelve pounds of bacon, three pounds of rice, some coffee and some sugar. They also brought along thirteen pints of roasted, finely ground corn; if they exhausted all their other supplies, they could eat spoonfuls of the cornmeal to stave off starvation. Their supplies lasted them just long enough to make it to Nashville, and they did eventually resort to eating their cornmeal.[78]

Natchez's earliest newspapers provide a look at what travelers could secure for provisions in the first years of the nineteenth century. As boat traffic downriver increased, traders from Ohio, Kentucky, Tennessee and Pennsylvania supplied Natchez and New Orleans with enormous quantities of flour; in the first six months of 1801, they delivered ninety-three thousand barrels of it. Ferdinand Claiborne, an early Natchez merchant, advertised in 1802 that he had the "best Monongahala flour," along with "a handsome and general assortment of merchandize."[79]

L. Valcourt, another merchant, advertised the kind of items that would have been luxurious—but also nonperishable—on the Trace. He had preserves, capers, anchovies, sugar from Havana, coffee and tea. And he sold alcoholic drinks: Jamaica rum and wines, brandies and gins from Europe. At the river landing, John Callender sold chocolate, pepper, allspice, mustard, green tea and cheese.[80]

In 1802, a list of commodities available in Natchez was published in the *Herald*. The list shows the staple foods that were available for purchase in Natchez, how much each item cost and how easy the items were to find. Bacon was 18.5 cents per pound and was "very scarce." Salt pork was $10 per barrel and was also scarce. Cornmeal was around $2.50 per barrel, and flour was $3 to $4 per barrel. Limes were plentiful. Madeira wine commanded the highest price for alcoholic drinks at $4 per gallon. Port was almost as expensive but was scarce.[81]

While plenty of stores (which often doubled as residences) existed in early Natchez, travelers could always purchase whole animals to slaughter and supply their trips, as Baily and his companions did in 1797 with their ox. And of course, travelers continued to draw on the same plants and animals that Indians had been exploiting for food for eons.

HUNTING AND FARMING

As Baily and his companions made their way up the Trace in 1797, they spotted potentially nourishing deer and turkeys. Armed only with pistols, and fearful of drawing unwanted attention from Creek raiders, they never killed any of the animals. But the Indians living near the Trace had been relying on those species as food for thousands of years.

To feed themselves prior to European contact, the tribes along the Natchez Trace relied on a hybridized lifestyle of hunting and gathering but also planting and harvesting. Most animal protein consumed by Indians was gotten by hunting, and the most important prey animal by far was the whitetail deer. It was the foundational animal that tribes along the Natchez Trace (and in the eastern woodlands generally) relied on for food, clothing and tools. From 50 to 90 percent of all animal protein consumed by southeastern Indians came from whitetail deer.[82]

Deer were a resilient species with a high reproductive rate that seemed so suited to Indian predation that one historian called them "semidomesticated." The Indian practice of burning underbrush on an annual basis meant that there were more open meadows for planting as well as for deer to graze on. Clearing the underbrush allowed deer to find chestnuts and acorns more easily too.[83]

Before European contact, Indians in the Southeast hunted with bow and arrow and relied on stealth to approach deer without being detected. A deer head decoy made of skin and antlers was one technique employed by hunters. Hunters would also use fire as a tool to corral deer; a group of hunters would encircle an area sometimes miles wide and set fire to fallen leaves. Panicked deer would be driven into the center of the circle.[84]

Bears were another large mammal preyed on by Indians along the Trace. Bears were scarce compared to deer, so they were not relied on as a food source. Rather, bears were valued for the oil that could be rendered from their fat. Soon after arriving in Natchez, John Blommart began trading with the local Choctaw for this oil.[85]

The wild turkey was an important game bird for Indians along the Trace, along with the passenger pigeon. In addition, southeastern Indians preyed on ducks, rabbits, squirrels, 'possums, raccoons, fish and frogs. Choctaw children were especially adept at taking small game with blowguns made of sections of hollowed-out cane. They were so skilled with the blowguns that they could regularly pierce animals' eyes with darts and were considered experts by the time they were ten years old.[86]

In addition to wild animal foods, the Southeast abounded with wild edible plants. Indians gathered several edible roots and drew on several species of fruits, most importantly the persimmon. Plums, muscadines, pawpaws, cherries, blackberries and raspberries were all native to the area and give an idea of some of the preserves L. Valcourt might have been selling at his store in 1801.

Indians along the Trace relied on many wild sources of food but also supplemented their diets with the "three sisters" crops: corn, beans and squash (which included pumpkins). They grew several varieties of each. The three native cultivars grew well in hot and humid conditions. Corn drew nitrogen from the soil, and beans replenished it. The crops each contributed essential nutrients to a healthy diet.

Sunflowers and bottle gourds were also important native cultivars, and Indians along the Trace grew other plants less well known today. Before European contact, Indians along the Trace did not keep domesticated turkeys, although like the whitetail deer, the wild version of the animal benefited from the burning of underbrush. They did keep domesticated dogs, and they sometimes ate them.[87]

When Europeans and southeastern Indians finally came into contact, the Columbian exchange began; Indians began adopting Old World plants and animals like chickens, pigs, cows and peaches, and Europeans began adopting New World plants and animals like turkeys, corn and tobacco. The diet that Indians, settlers and travelers along the Natchez Trace relied on around the turn of the nineteenth century was a combination of two worlds' staples.

The Chickasaw Nation around that time was an example of this kind of mixed-world agricultural lifestyle. One traveler who passed through the nation via the Trace in 1803 described a landscape very different from that of the wilderness of the central portion of the road. Near Tockshish, settled by John McIntosh prior to the American Revolution, the traveler saw lots of horses, cows and pigs. He passed a gristmill and many fields of corn fenced in and well maintained. He noted that there were a lot of white settlers along this section of the Trace and that they got along well with the Chickasaw. The Chickasaw made money by selling the traveler the "best cured and sweet bacon we found on the road."[88]

STANDS

It didn't take long for other savvy businesspeople—and those who had simply settled near the Trace and were therefore well positioned—to realize that there was money to be made selling food, supplies and lodging to travelers. In 1797, when Baily and his party made their journey, a few settlements existed in the Chickasaw Nation and on the Trace closer to Natchez; most of the path, though, ran through wilderness. Three years later, the push to tame the entire Trace began in earnest when the Trace was designated a post road by the U.S. government.

Winthrop Sargent, the first governor of the Mississippi Territory, expressed a desire to see taverns opened a day's ride apart along the entire road. The taverns, which would come to be called "stands," would supply travelers with basic food and drink, fodder for horses and a place to sleep—sometimes only a place to camp.

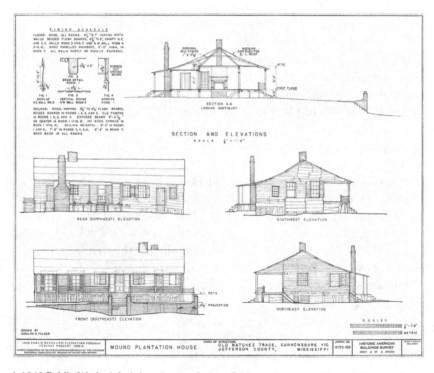

A 1940 Public Works Administration rendering of Mount Locust, or Mound Plantation, as it was sometimes called. *Library of Congress.*

Choctaw and Chickasaw leaders were reluctant to allow taverns along the Trace, but by 1805—the year after Lorenzo Dow's provisions were washed away in the Pearl River—they had relented, and new stands began to open in their nations. The men who opened the stands were "countrymen," white men who had married Indian women and had lived in the Indian nations for long periods of time or the mixed-race children of whites and Indians. The opening of the stands facilitated an immense increase in the number of travelers using the Trace. By 1815, twenty-three stands existed in the Choctaw and Chickasaw Nations.[89]

In the beginning, stands were rough and spartan. The nicer ones, like Mount Locust sixteen miles north of Natchez, offered fresh supplies from its adjoining farm, sturdy accommodations (so sturdy that the building still stands today, the oldest frame building in Mississippi), corn shuck mattresses and a taproom. Even with two floors of wall-to-wall mattresses, Mount Locust still allowed travelers to camp on its grounds.[90]

The not-so-nice stands could provide only the most basic of accommodations. Reverend Thomas Nixon famously described an "Indian hotel" he stayed at while traveling the Trace in 1815. His room was constructed from small poles and had a dirt floor. The roof of the building was just tall enough for him to stand up. The only accoutrement in the room was a bearskin that served as a sleeping mat; some rooms lacked even the bearskins. "You feel blank and disappointed when you find a cold dirt floor, blank walls, and no fire," he wrote.[91]

As more people traveled the Trace in the early 1800s, the quality of stands improved. Trace historian Tony L. Turnbow has studied unpublished documents describing the stands of the Trace and conveyed to the authors of this book a more complete picture of Natchez Trace accommodation than what is widely known:

When Jefferson approved building public stands in 1804, the Army oversaw building and leasing public stands that I think were of a higher standard. They built the inn at Colbert's Ferry, and the photo of that building from the early 1900s matches the design of the inn at Gordon's Ferry in Tennessee also shown in a photo. Norton's was a public stand near the Pearl River that the War Department leased. I suspect they also built the building.

[James] Robertson described Young Factor's as a "Fine House of Entertainment," and by 1819, when the two post riders that bought it battled in court, their list of assets included fine furnishings, crystal

goblets, and china. The Choctaw Agency house that Dinsmore operated as an inn was a two-story brick building, and Turner Brashear's Stand in the Choctaw Nation was a two story building made from heavy cypress logs. He also operated a racecourse for horses there. Louis LeFleur's French Camp also seems to have been a two-story log structure. He had a colorful woven carpet on the floor. Allen's Tavern in present-day Kosciusko was also a two-story structure.[92]

Turner Brashears and his brother Eden both operated stands along the Trace—Eden near the border between the Natchez District and the Choctaw Nation and Turner about forty miles into the Choctaw Nation. Both men advertised their stands in Natchez's *Mississippi Messenger*. Turner Brashears offered "provender and provision" and operated a blacksmith shop at his stand. Eden's advertisement was more specific; he offered corn, bacon, whiskey and biscuit baked fresh daily.[93]

Fresh-baked biscuits and bacon must have been especially enticing to travelers who had stayed at less accommodating stands along the road. Food at some stands straddled the nexus between nourishing, boring and revolting.

Pork was the most common meat offered at stands, but some offered beef, venison and dried fish as well. Corn was ever present as an item on stand menus and as fodder for horses. One corn dish mentioned by travelers was "sour hominy." Episcopal bishop Robert Roberts ate the dish traveling north on the Trace in 1816. To make it, ground corn was treated with lye and left in water for long enough to begin fermenting. A visitor to the Cherokee Nation described the food as a staple among the Indians, but it was the worst-tasting thing they ate, in his opinion.[94]

Cornbread was another dish served at stands. Unlike the modern cornbread familiar to southerners, it was not the fluffy, buttery yellow loaf leavened with baking powder. Instead, cornbread made in the Indian fashion incorporated all the

Tomb of Eden Brashear, Grand Gulf, Mississippi. *Ryan Starrett.*

"three sisters" crops. The bread was made of boiled corn smashed together with beans and roasted pumpkins.[95]

Weary travelers who had been subsisting on sour hominy, salted meat and the like along the road would find a sumptuous array waiting for them in Natchez—if they had the money to pay for it. By 1822, more and better groceries were available for travelers to purchase. In addition to the old staples of bacon, corn, flour and rum, shoppers could also buy apples, prime beef and pork, molasses, sugar grown in Louisiana, cognac, peach brandy and venison hams.[96]

A couple of businessmen named Vaughan and King opened a bar in Natchez in 1819 and announced in verse the luxuries they were prepared to offer patrons, for the right price:

> *A Bar-room is now ready,*
> *Where wine and cider there shall be,*
> *And porter too, with ale for thee,*
> *As good as any in the town,*
> *And punch so strong 'twill lay you down,*
> *A ham, and tongues, if't can be had,*
> *And venison, too, to make you glad,*
> *Gin, cigars, cheese, lemonade, and whiskey,*
> *Biscuits, bitters and brandy, to make you frisky,*
> *Sangaree, mint sling, cherry-bounce and toddy,*
> *Here you may drink 'til your head goes niddy noddy*[97]

Of course, as enticing as Vaughan and King's advertisement would have been to travelers ending their journey in Natchez, the businessmen were most likely hoping to attract the Kaintucks, flush with cash from selling their wheat and goods, who were preparing to depart for a journey up the Trace back to Ohio or Kentucky or Tennessee.

A Kaintuck sitting down at Vaughan and King's to a dinner of venison ham, sweet potato mash, fresh greens and pudding would have an idea of the impoverished days that lay ahead on the Trace. But with enough glasses of porter consumed—and perhaps a mint sling or toddy thrown in—his mind would have ascended to a land of tingling pleasure for a few hours. The liquor would have helped him sleep, before an early morning start down a long and impoverished road.

Chapter 7

WAR ON THE TRACE

THE CHICKASAW CAMPAIGN OF 1736, THE WAR OF 1812 AND THE CIVIL WAR

No man is so foolish as to desire war more than peace:
for in peace sons bury their fathers, but in war fathers bury their sons.
—Herodotus[98]

ACKIA

Jean-Baptiste Le Moyne de Bienville was back. The man who was responsible for the French settlement of the Gulf Coast had been sent back from France for a second tour of duty. Since his absence in 1728, things had gone poorly for his replacement. Of particular consternation to the French government was the massacre of 235 French men, women and children at the hands of the Natchez in 1729. While the French had exacted a terrible revenge on the Natchez, the remnants of that tribe had been absorbed by the Chickasaw Nation. The Chickasaw refusal to hand over the remaining Natchez caused France to authorize the destruction of the former nation.

A plan was concocted whereby Bienville would march north at the head of more than five hundred French soldiers and mercenaries, along with forty-five African slaves. They would recruit Choctaw warriors along the way to supplement their ranks. Meanwhile, Pierre d'Artaguette, commander of the Illinois District, would march south from Illinois at the head of a coalition of French and Indians. The two forces would meet on March 31 and settle the Chickasaw menace once and for all, thereby uniting French Louisiana with French Canada.

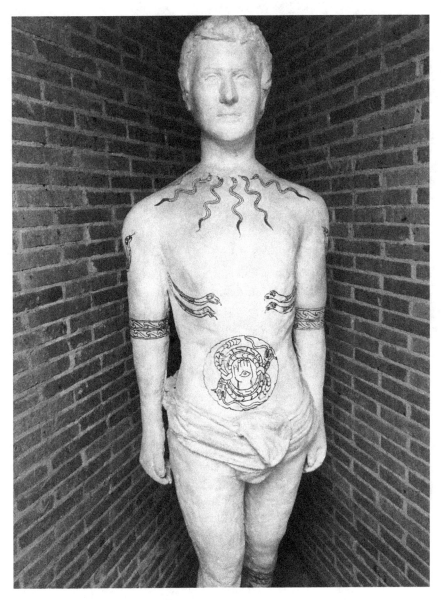

A representation of Bienville's tattoos. *Ryan Starrett.*

The French would own the lion's share of North America. All that stood in the way was one native nation.[99]

Bienville was a master at both Indian diplomacy and warfare. He spoke four native languages, knew how to use the carrot and the stick and, most importantly, had the respect—or at least the fear—of the surrounding tribes. Three decades of frontier conditions on the Gulf Coast and its interior had turned the governor into a hardened and pragmatic frontiersman. He was known to fight in the buff, native style, and had a mosaic of native and Christian symbols tattooed across his body, including numerous snakes. He was equally prepared to smoke the calumet or wield the musket.[100] As usual in 1736, he offered the former to the Choctaw. He would bring the latter to the Chickasaw.

BIENVILLE DID, IN FACT, pick up Choctaw auxiliaries along the way. He added six hundred warriors to his command by distributing gifts and promising a reward for each Chickasaw scalp collected during the campaign. The combined force arrived outside the village of Chikasahha on May 22, 1736.[101] Bienville built a base for his boats and supplies and continued northwest two days later. After a two-day march, his army arrived at the village of Ackia.[102] The Chickasaw were waiting—just like they had been awaiting D'Artaguette two months before.

D'ARTAGUETTE HAD ARRIVED AT Chickasaw Bluff[103] with 140 French soldiers and 266 Indian allies—Iroquois, Arkansas, Miamis and Illinois. Instead of rendezvousing with the other French force, he received a letter from Mobile stating that Bienville had been delayed. D'Artaguette now found himself in a difficult position. It could be a month or more before Bienville reached the rendezvous. D'Artaguette's army was predominantly Indian, and he didn't have enough food and supplies to keep them in the field for a protracted amount of time. Consequently, he developed a new plan: he would attack a nearby Chickasaw village,[104] use its supplies to keep his army in the field and throw up fortifications around the village for protection until Bienville arrived. The elimination of the Chickasaw would simply have to wait a month.

On March 25, Palm Sunday, the French and their allies rapidly and confidently marched toward their target. When they got to within a mile of the village, D'Artaguette left thirty men behind to guard the baggage and

The Bienville statue in New Orleans. *Ryan Starrett.*

moved in for the kill. His mission was a complete success. He was nearly at the village and had taken it by surprise. All that remained was to dispose of the surprised villagers.

D'Artaguette's troops quickly captured several fortified houses, but then the others began to resist. Not long after being bogged down in a house-to-house fight, nearly five hundred Chickasaw stormed down a neighboring hill on D'Artaguette's flank. Most of his Indian allies fled immediately. D'Artaguette tried desperately to fight his way back to his supply depot. Roughly sixty Arkansas and Iroquois remained with him, but it was not enough. D'Artaguette was severely wounded three times and captured along with twenty comrades, including the Jesuit priest, Father Antoninus Senat.

The few surviving Frenchmen made their way hastily back to the Illinois territory, dispatching an urgent message to Bienville along the way. It never arrived.

Later that afternoon, nineteen of the captives, including D'Artaguette and Father Senat, were burned at the stake. Their Palm Sunday march into Ogoula Tchetoka had been greeted not with cheers and adulation but with shrieks and war cries. Father Senat proposed to his companions that they enter another kingdom as martyrs—and along the way show the Chickasaw that Frenchmen, too, could die bravely. He then marched into the flames unassisted.[105]

TWO MONTHS LATER, ON May 26, outside Ackia, Bienville still had no news of D'Artaguette. Nevertheless, he decided to go ahead and attack.

Again, the Chickasaw were ready. Having taken papers off D'Artaguette (and having them translated by English traders/advisors), they knew that Bienville would be approaching shortly.[106] They promptly began fortifying their villages. They did so by putting up palisades and digging a trench behind them shoulder deep. They would then shoot through ground-level loopholes at approaching foes. In addition, their cabins were scattered to create a multitude of crossfires.

However, Bienville's army was significantly larger that D'Artaguette's. Bienville had more than 1,200 men at his disposal, evenly split between Europeans and Choctaw. A little more than 100 Chickasaw and a handful of English advisors opposed him. Despite the lack of cannons, Bienville ordered the attack. His men stormed the hill and quickly took the first cabin under a withering fire. Then they took a second, but the Chickasaw poured down such devastating volleys from their remaining cabins and fort that the

ACKIA 1736

Cast aluminum door panels at the Mississippi War Memorial Building, commemorating the Battle of Ackia. *Joseph Starrett.*

French became bogged down. Their officers urged them on to the fort, but the rank and file refused to move from behind the two cabins they had taken. The officers, in advance of their men, urged them to be brave and act like Frenchmen. They refused. At that moment, four French officers fell almost simultaneously. One of them sent an aide to rally the troops still taking cover. He was shot dead before he got to the cabin. His death convinced those who were taking shelter to continue to do so.

To make matters worse, the Choctaw had fired one covering volley from the base of the hill and then withdrawn out of range of the Chickasaw guns.

With his Indian allies taking cover at a safe distance and his countrymen mired down in front of a fort they could not take, Bienville ordered a retreat. The French gathered as many of their wounded as they could and hastened to their base on the Tombigbee River. They arrived six days later and continued until they reached Mobile.

Bienville suffered two hundred French casualties and roughly two dozen Choctaw casualties. And he left behind a victorious, undefeated Chickasaw Nation.

ANDREW JACKSON AND THE TENNESSEE VOLUNTEERS

1813

Major General James Wilkinson—once the highest-ranking general in the U.S. Army—was going to ruin Andrew Jackson. He would do so by killing as many of Jackson's Tennessee Volunteers as he could.

The charismatic and corpulent Wilkinson was a poor field commander but an excellent politician. He was the definition *par excellence* of a political general who ruled a bona fide fiefdom in the American Southwest from his capital, New Orleans. He was "a general who never won a battle or lost a court-martial."[107]

Despite having been a member of the Conway Cabal, which tried to replace George Washington as commander-in-chief, Wilkinson managed to work his way back into the good graces of his country. His run of luck continued when his patron, Thomas Jefferson, became the third president of the United States. Jefferson was a westward-looking president who trusted Wilkinson and made him the governor of the Louisiana Territory, in addition to being the senior-ranking military commander. It was not enough for Wilkinson. The man of whom Theodore Roosevelt would write, "In all our history, there is no more despicable character,"[108] wanted more. A lot more. Wilkinson entered the services of Spain as Agent 13. He spent the next two decades ruthlessly pursuing land, fame, money and power. And he was prepared to eliminate anyone who got in his way.[109]

In 1790, President Washington sent fifteen soldiers under the command of Major John Doughty to meet with the southern tribes and to eventually establish a military base at the mouth of Bear Creek and the Tennessee River. Wilkinson promptly informed the Spanish and suggested they eliminate the American party. Spain's Indian allies ambushed the troops, killing five and wounding six.[110]

"The Pioneer," by Thomas Nast.
Library of Congress.

James Wilkinson. *Library of Congress.*

In 1804, he warned Spain about the Lewis and Clark Expedition. He even recommended that Spain intercept the explorers with an armed guard—in which case Lewis and Clark would be remembered by a select few as two early adventurers who disappeared in the West.[111]

And then there was the incident at Terre aux Boeufs and Cantonment Washington.

Andrew Jackson was determined to lead an army, ideally against the British. Having been struck in the head by a British officer when he was thirteen, Jackson carried a scar and a grudge the rest of his life. When war erupted with Britain in 1812, he leaped at the opportunity to settle an old score. He quickly raised an army of 1,500 infantry and set sail down the Cumberland, Ohio and Mississippi Rivers and then down to New Orleans. He sent a second detachment of 600 cavalry under Colonel John Coffee down the Natchez Trace.

Although he was a major general in charge of more than two thousand militia troops—the Tennessee Volunteers—and on the march to fight the British, Jackson was not entirely satisfied with his assignment. He had preferred to wrest control of East Florida from His Royal Majesty or even fight the redcoats along the Canadian border. He did not want to be sent to the Gulf Department. True, New Orleans was the obvious choice for a concerted British attack, but there was one, inescapable deterrent to Jackson's ambitions on the Gulf Coast: James Wilkinson.

Wilkinson was a general in the regular U.S. Army. Being a general of militia, Jackson would be expected to serve under Wilkinson. The glory of defeating Britain—or capturing Mobile or Pensacola—would therefore go to Wilkinson, whom Jackson despised. For years, the crusty Tennessean had suspected Wilkinson of double-dealing with Spain but could never prove it.

Rather than report with his troops to New Orleans, Jackson decided to remain near Natchez. He marched his army six miles east to the town of Washington, where he planned to establish an encampment at Cantonment Washington, nearly two hundred miles from Wilkinson.[112] When Jackson's troops arrived on February 17, just as darkness began to descend on the winter-white Spanish moss, they were greeted by an ominous sight: more than three hundred tombstones.

1809

On October 31, 1809, General Wilkinson arrived at Cantonment Washington with 1,107 soldiers, 617 of whom were ill. Most had become sick when he set up a camp outside New Orleans at Terre aux Boeufs. The camp quickly became a breeding ground for more disease as the soldiers relieved themselves wherever they liked, including the levee where they got their drinking water. "Drainage ditches and culverts became refuse dumps, filled with 'stinking meat...vegetables, old clothes, and every species of filth.'" Wilkinson was ordered by the War Department to move to Washington, Mississippi, on the Natchez Trace. He did so, and three months later, another 326 would be dead.

Two years later, Wilkinson was court-martialed for allowing eight hundred troops to die on his watch. He was acquitted on all charges and rewarded by being made a major general and sent back to his fiefdom in New Orleans.[113]

1813

Nearly a month after arriving at Cantonment Washington, Jackson was informed that one of his trumpeters, Benjamin Darnell, had died. Jackson ordered a coffin constructed and Darnell to be buried with full military honors. The sound of the coffin being built, the troops marching and the final salvo fired over his tomb could be heard by all the troops at the cantonment, including the 150 sick, 56 of whom could not even walk to the funeral.[114]

The next day, John Wise succumbed to sickness. He, too, was buried with full military honors. It was the third such funeral in four days. Time was running out on Jackson—just as Wilkinson plotted.

And then came the ultimate blow: Andrew Jackson and the Tennessee Volunteers were ordered by the War Department to disband and return home. They were to hand their equipment over to Wilkinson and make the four-hundred-plus-mile trek through Indian territory and the wilderness as best they could—no wagons, no tents and no arms. The growing number of sick pleaded with Jackson not to abandon them as their country had. Seeing the hopelessness of the situation, Jackson went to his tent and wept.[115]

On March 6, 1813, Jackson addressed his troops.

> *The Major Genl having pledged himself that he would never abandon one of his men and that he would act the part of a father to them has to repeat that he will not leave one of the sick nor of the detachment behind. He has led you here. He will lead you back to your country and friends. The sick as far as he has the power and means shall be made comfortable. If any one dies, he will pay to them the last tribute of respect. They shall be buried with all honors of war. Should your General die, he knows it is a respect you will pay to him. It is a debt due to every honest soldier of the detachment.*[116]

Andrew Jackson was determined to march his Volunteers home to Tennessee. Not one would be left behind to die a solitary death. All casualties along the way would be buried with full military honors.

The next four weeks were an odyssey through hell. With scarce supplies, a growing list of invalids and a more than four-hundred-mile journey ahead, Jackson held his troops together through force of will alone. Early on, he dismounted his horse and gave it to a sick soldier. Thenceforth, the aging general, battling his own sickness, would walk with his men.

A few fell along the way. Thomas Taylor, who was left behind at Pigeon Roost and moved to French Camp, died at four o'clock in the morning on March 26. All, including Jackson, certainly endured intense hunger, fear and suffering. Near the end of the trek, one of his men was bitten by a rattlesnake while waiting to cross the Tennessee River. Fortunately, he survived.[117] In fact, nearly all of Jackson's two thousand men made it back to their homes.[118]

INSTEAD OF THE COURT-MARTIAL he feared, instead of public humiliation and contempt, Andrew Jackson was greeted as a hero when he returned to Nashville. The crusty general had led his "sons" home. Far fewer would have returned had Jackson not insisted on leaving no man behind.

The Tennessee Volunteers rewarded their general with the moniker "Old Hickory," and many of them marched with him again in 1814 to New Orleans, where Jackson decisively defeated the British in one of the most lopsided and important battles in U.S. history.

Forever after, Andrew Jackson was associated with New Orleans. But it was on the Natchez Trace that he cut his chops and proved his ability to lead an army. It was on the Natchez Trace that his legend was born.

FIVE DAYS IN MAY: GRANT MORTALLY WOUNDS THE CONFEDERACY

Raymond, Mississippi, May 12, 1863

Grant's XVII Corps, twelve thousand strong, under James McPherson overran Confederate general Gregg's four thousand men at Raymond, located between Vicksburg and Jackson. The "skirmish" led to one thousand casualties, evenly divided between the two sides. Yet an even casualty count always favored the Federals, who could draw on reinforcements while the Confederacy could not. In addition, the battle made Grant determined to wipe out Mississippi's capital, Jackson, before applying his death grip to Vicksburg.

Jackson, Mississippi, May 14, 1863

Mississippi's capital city was in ruins. Factories, warehouses, railroads and homes were destroyed. Much of the city was burned to the ground. Jefferson Davis's home state was, in effect, conquered. Now Grant determined to vanquish the heart of the Confederacy.

Champion Hill, Mississippi, May 16, 1863

General John Pemberton was ordered to attack Grant's rear in Clinton and then join forces with CSA general Joseph Johnston. Knowing that he was outnumbered two to one, Pemberton instead set up a defensive

Series of illustrations of the Battle of Raymond from *Harper's Weekly*. *Library of Congress.*

position around Champion Hill. Soon, the Federal troops arrived, and not wanting to give the Rebels extra time to improve their defenses, Grant ordered an immediate attack. At first, it seemed a terrible mistake, as the Rebel troops repulsed and then drove a dangerous wedge between the Federal army. However, Confederate general William Loring—who could have delivered the decisive blow with his reinforcements—was nowhere to be found. Instead, he was leading his men on a long route along back trails. When he finally arrived, the battle was over and Pemberton was in full retreat toward Vicksburg.

It was left to the tardy Loring to cover that retreat. He passed the assignment to General Lloyd Tilghman, the popular general who, a year before, had led the bulk of his outmatched army at Fort Henry to safety and then returned to surrender with the skeleton crew he had left behind. Half a year later, Tilghman was part of a prisoner exchange and returned to a command in the Confederate army. Now he was tasked with saving Pemberton's army.

Tilghman rode to his front lines, where he sent his son with a squad to drive out a nest of Federal sharpshooters. He himself then adjusted the sights on one of his cannons. As he watched through his field glasses, a Federal shell tore through his abdomen and side, killing the horse behind him instantly.

General Tilghman breathed on, but not for long. Sergeant E.T. Eggleston would later report:

> *It was some little time after the general fell before his son, a youth, could be found, and I shall never forget the touching scene when the grief and lamentations he cast himself on his dying and unconscious father. Those of us who witnessed this distressing scene shed tears of sympathy, for the bereaved son and of sorrow for our fallen hero, the chivalrous and beloved Tilghman.*[119]

In his official report, Loring would credit Tilghman with holding off a force that outnumbered him five to one. "He not only haled them in check, but repulsed him on several occasions, and this kept open the only line of retreat left to the army. The bold stand of his brigade under the lamented hero saved a large portion of the army."[120]

Tilghman's body was carried to Vicksburg, where he was buried with full military honors.

Grave of Robert Cooper. *Ryan Starrett.*

CAPTAIN ROBERT THEODORE COOPER had been paroled just six months before the Vicksburg Campaign, having been captured at Fort Donelson in February 1862. Six months as a Federal prisoner did not alter his devotion to the Confederacy. Upon release, he promptly rejoined his comrades and fought at the Battle of Champion Hill. Like General Tilghman, Captain Cooper would also give his life on the hill.[121]

His father, Robert Melville Cooper, had another son to bury. Ten of his eleven sons had enlisted in the Confederate army. Only one would return home unscathed. The patriarch had built the coffin for and identified the remains of Meriwether Lewis; fought with Andrew Jackson at the Battle of New Orleans; served his country as a teacher, businessman and circuit court clerk; lost his nurse wife in a Confederate hospital; and now had another child to bury.[122]

Vicksburg, Mississippi, May 18

The anaconda began to coil around its prey. Its prize was free roam of the Mississippi River, the Amazon of the North. He came into existence when General Winfield Scott unveiled his grand strategy before Abraham Lincoln back in 1861. He began to awaken when the cannons roared along the Natchez Trace at Raymond. He started to uncoil at Jackson. He prepared to strike at Champion Hill. He wrapped his powerful body around Vicksburg. And then he squeezed, tighter and tighter—so tight that the Confederacy was strangled to death.

During the five days from May 12 to May 16, 1863, eight thousand Federal and Confederate troops were killed or wounded. Thousands more would die during the Siege of Vicksburg. But with the fall of Vicksburg, the end of the Civil War was a foregone conclusion. Grant's five-day campaign and subsequent siege made it so.

Chapter 8

AGES OF BANDITS

THE MEN WHO TOOK

MASTER OF THE CHICKASAW, 1780s

The old man squinted from the thickness of the woods. Making its way upriver was his prize: a keelboat bound for St. Louis. His contacts in Natchez had informed him of the boat's arrival, and now here he was, perfectly positioned to claim it. He needed the boat to approach the shore, though, so he and his companions could get their hands on its moorings.

To bring the boat in, the old man had planned a ruse. A companion fluent in French would call out to the important woman on board, "Madame Anicanora Ramos—*j'ai du courrier pour toi*! Mrs. Anicanora Ramos, I have some mail for you!"

The keelboat carried clothes, liquor, gunpowder and money. Depriving the Spanish of the cargo would be sweet. But the real prize was Ramos, the twenty-seven-year-old wife of the Spanish governor of St. Louis, Francisco Cruzat.

Ramos bought the ruse. Her keelboat pulled ashore, and the old man rushed out of the woods with forty British compatriots bearing rifles, tomahawks and knives. The keelboat was his. Ramos was his. After searching the boat, he realized that he had captured not only the wife of the Spanish governor but also their four children. Even better—the Spanish would be forced to meet the old man's demands. Soon Captain John Blommart, the liberator of Natchez, would be free again.

Ramos must have realized quickly that she had been captured that day in 1782 by an infamous old man. His name was James Logan Colbert, and

Contadina Family Prisoners with Banditti, painted by Edward Smith, circa the 1820s to the 1840s. *Smithsonian American Art Museum.*

he was at the center of the convergence of nations occurring in the lower Mississippi Valley in the late 1700s.[123]

Colbert was a Carolinian of Scottish ancestry, but he was also deeply Chickasaw. He had been with the tribe since his childhood, living the life of an Indian during a time when Indians still held dominion over the Southeast. By the time Anicanora Ramos came paddling up the river near present-day Memphis, Colbert had been living with the Chickasaw for more than forty years.

He had proven to be a brave warrior. He had married three Chickasaw women and fathered a host of children. Perhaps most important to his ascent to power, he had used his position as an English-speaking Carolinian to deepen the powerful alliance that Great Britain had cultivated with the Chickasaw Nation over the course of most of the past century.[124]

For the previous three years, Colbert had used his position as a master of the Chickasaw domain to attack the enemies of the British king: the Spanish and Americans who threatened British hegemony in the Southeast. The capture of Ramos would secure the freedom of John Blommart, the old

British sea captain who had captured Natchez from the Spanish with the help of an army of Choctaw and Creek Indians, only to surrender it back when British reinforcements never arrived.

But Colbert was not only concerned with the king's interests in the Southeast; his raids on the Spanish were also payback for what he perceived as mistreatment by Spanish soldiers in the lower Mississippi Valley who had taken Chickasaw furs and charged exorbitant prices for trade goods. The British considered him a military leader, but the Spanish considered him a bandit and a pirate.[125]

A few days after Ramos's capture, one of Colbert's sons arrived at their camp, along with three hundred Chickasaw warriors. There was much talk about what should be done with Ramos and her children. Some wanted them marched into the Chickasaw homeland. The main Chickasaw settlements lay astride the Natchez Trace near present-day Tupelo, Mississippi. The Trace was an important trading path in those days, but one seldom used by Europeans. A few decades later, the Trace would become known as the hunting grounds of highwaymen. Ironically, Colbert would have considered the Trace a refuge; it was the world outside the Trace that needed to fear him and his Chickasaw raiders.

The thought of disappearing one hundred miles into the southeastern interior must have terrified Ramos. And it must have been a great relief when Colbert told her that after three weeks of captivity, she and her children would be released and allowed to sail downriver to Spanish New Orleans. Colbert gave her a letter, in which he asked the Spanish governor at New Orleans, Estevan Miro, to free Blommart (he eventually did).[126]

Following their surrender to the Americans, the British evacuated the Carolinas later that year, and Colbert and the Chickasaw Nation found themselves forced to reckon with a new, homegrown imperial power. Within a few years, the Chickasaw would find themselves loyal and valued allies of the Cumberland River settlers and the United States. But Colbert would have to leave the engineering of that alliance to his progeny; he was thrown from his horse and killed in 1784.

THE TICK, 1800–1803

John Swaney bounced along the single-track trail, through Chickasaw country, through Choctaw country, from Natchez to Nashville, from Nashville to Natchez, week after week. His life was a paradox; he spent most of his time isolated, riding the Trace, carrying the mail. But he was also one of the few men to know—and connect—two important early American cities, as well as the people who lived in and between them.

Swaney knew everyone on the Trace in those final years of the eighteenth century. The men and women he passed on his never-ending trips were always one of three things: Indians, settlers (there were very few of them in those days) or traders making their way up from Natchez after a trip down the Mississippi River. So it must have been jarring to Swaney when a new man showed up on the Trace who was none of those things.

The man was near sixty years old and had the grizzled look of someone who had spent his life on the frontier. He was lean and strong and wore buckskin clothes. He hung around with a few others, younger than him. They had the same look. The man took a particular interest in Swaney and hailed him for a chat whenever he saw him riding by.

Swaney learned that the new man's name was Samuel Mason. And he must have surmised early on that this Mason fellow was dangerous.

Like the ticks that waited on leaves all along the Trace for deer to brush past and provide a ride and a blood meal, Mason too had positioned himself. His hosts would be the river traders who had begun to appear more and more frequently in the previous decade—the traders who traveled up the Trace toward Nashville with all their money in their horses' saddlebags or sewn into their clothes. Soon Swaney would begin hearing stories of river traders being robbed along the Trace. Soon, he would even find Mason's victims himself, cowering in the woods, robbed of everything they owned.

Mason's life had begun farther north, in the backcountry. Like his father, who had moved his family from Norfolk, Virginia, to the West Virginia frontier, Mason saw opportunity in the West. He became a landowner and militia captain early in life. During the American Revolution, Mason distinguished himself as an Indian fighter and leader. Afterward, he kept a tavern and farmed at present-day Wheeling, West Virginia, on the Ohio River. Mason was poised to become a respectable pillar of American settlement in the West. But he had a problem: he didn't like working and didn't mind stealing.

Mason took up with a group of "louts" and began burglarizing houses. His own general ordered him out of the country, and he fled to the Kentucky frontier, where he further "deteriorated." Removed from the laws of settled society, Mason began to act like the outlaw he would become—stealing, leading a gang to beat the local constable nearly to death after a personal slight, kidnapping a Black family and rejecting sexual and familial norms.

Three bandits preparing to bury their stolen money. From *The Banditti of the Prairies*, 1856. *Internet Archive.*

Mason and his family developed a reputation for preying on travelers in Kentucky and were likely responsible for multiple murders, including sniping as he crossed a river the same constable Mason had nearly beaten to death before. It didn't take long for the Mason family to be driven further from the settlements.

Mason moved south to Cave-in-Rock on the Ohio River, where he practiced river piracy. He likely spent the next three years robbing travelers on the Ohio and Mississippi Rivers before moving yet farther south, to the Natchez Trace.

A story related later by Swaney gives an insight into the tactics Mason and his men used to prey on traders along the Trace. One night a group of "Kaintucks," as they were called, made camp at Gum Springs in the Choctaw Nation. After kindling their fires, the men were preparing to sleep.

The Kaintucks didn't realize that Mason and his men, their faces blackened, were silently creeping through the grass toward them. When one of the traders' pickets accidentally stepped on a Mason man, the ambush was sprung. One of the bandits fired his gun and shouted, "Kill every boatman." The traders were so terrified that they fled into the woods in their nightclothes.

Swaney, the mail carrier, rode up on the men's ransacked camp the next morning and realized that something was wrong. He blew a bugle, and the traders gradually trickled out of the woods and told Swaney what had happened. They resolved to arm themselves with clubs, track the Mason men and get their possessions back. They followed the trail, finding a pair of pants with four Spanish doubloons sewn inside that the Mason men had overlooked. They made it two miles before the Mason gang again ambushed them from the cover of the woods. Their courage failing, the traders fled once more, eventually using the four doubloons to get themselves back home.

Mason carried out his depredations on the Trace and then the Mississippi River for three more years, galvanizing the entire southwestern frontier against him. Eventually, a $1,000 bounty on Mason tempted two of his own gang members to split his head with a tomahawk in Jefferson County, Mississippi, and to then sever the head and bring it, rolled in clay, to Natchez. Rather than receiving a reward, the two men were hanged shortly after.[127]

The Illusionist, 1997–2002

Bernie Ebbers had never minded the attention. His height, at six-feet-four, had drawn the eyes of his community growing up in Edmonton, Alberta. And he had never minded conflict. In fact, he relished it. He had distinguished himself as a basketball player, combining an unusual aggressiveness with his size. "If someone was in his way," a friend would tell a reporter years later, "he would run them over."[128]

A chance application—and the subsequent offer of a basketball scholarship—brought Ebbers to Mississippi College in Clinton, Mississippi. Ebbers found himself relocated 1,900 miles to a town and campus that sat on an old Indian trail: the Natchez Trace. And it was there that he would settle permanently, employing his competitive instincts to become an entrepreneur and a billionaire. He bought a motel and then a string of motels. He started a telecom company, which would come to be known as WorldCom. Then he bought dozens of other telecom companies. He offered MCI, the second-largest telecom company in the United States, more than $36 billion to become his. When MCI accepted the offer and Ebbers became the chief executive of the largest internet traffic provider in the world, all of a sudden Ebbers got *all* the attention. Readers of the *New York Times* opened their newspaper on October 2, 1997, to see his smiling face—the Canadian from Mississippi with the shaggy hair, gray beard and toothy smile. The "Long-Distance Visionary," the *Times* called him. Fifty-nine thousand MCI employees had a new boss, and he conducted his business from Clinton, Mississippi.

Ebbers's offer for MCI had been audacious and unexpected. And he was able to make the offer by doing what he had been doing for more than a decade: taking on debt and using shares of his company as the medium of purchase rather than cash. Ebbers would use WorldCom shares to buy a company. The shares would rise in value. He would use those now more valuable shares to buy another company. The shares would rise in value again. Of the $36.5 billion WorldCom offered MCI, $30 billion was in WorldCom shares.

It was a strategy that seemed to facilitate limitless expansion. In 1997, the *New York Times* called the practice "a cycle that feeds voraciously on itself." Within five years, it would become clear that the cycle had not just fed on itself but devoured itself, a black hole sucking in all surrounding light.[129]

For a few years, though, Ebbers was a hero in Mississippi and a celebrity in the business world. Ebbers headquartered his company in Clinton and raised $100 million for Mississippi College. Professionals in downtown Jackson would watch him emerge from a restaurant at lunchtime wearing jeans and a cowboy hat and think, "He can walk on water."[130]

The year after the MCI-WorldCom merger, Ebbers invited a reporter to interview him in surroundings fitting of a businessman who seemed able to conjure billions of dollars from the humid Mississippi air. The reporter met Ebbers on his yacht, *Countach*, floating outside Hilton Head, South Carolina. MCI-WorldCom was sponsoring a PGA tournament there.

The reporter must have been impressed as he stepped aboard the yacht; it was 132 feet long, with multiple sleek levels of white fiberglass and black windows. It had five large staterooms, ten bathrooms, a gym and a hot tub. It was decked, trimmed and paneled with teakwood. A local South Carolinian described it to a reporter as "something out of Star Trek, sitting on the water."[131]

Ebbers fondled a cigar and told the reporter how he wasn't afraid to delegate responsibilities to his subordinates. "People that have problems admitting what they don't know are people who get in a world of trouble," Ebbers told the reporter. One of the men aboard that day was Scott Sullivan, Ebbers's chief financial officer. A few years later, Ebbers would argue that he had delegated MCI-WorldCom's accounting to Sullivan—that it was Sullivan who had acted alone, without Ebbers's knowledge.

In the end, it was the self-devouring cycle of acquisitions that would bring about Ebbers's demise. Up to then, Ebbers's success had been built on those ever-rising WorldCom stock prices. In 2000, Ebbers hoped to once again dramatically expand the size of his company by purchasing Sprint for

$145 billion. He hoped that the deal would once again stimulate WorldCom stock prices, which had begun to decline in previous months. But the Justice Department blocked the deal, saying that the new merger would harm competition in the telecommunications industry.

Ebbers's strategy of acquisitions had reached its terminus. Now he would be forced, as a reporter put it, to "figure out how to grow the company by running a better, more innovative business."[132]

Ebbers's numerous acquisitions (he had purchased sixty-five companies up to that point) had provided an illusion of profitability for years; now Ebbers needed to show that his company could grow its stock price based on a more old-fashioned metric of business success: earnings. And if he could not show high earnings, WorldCom stock prices would continue to fall, bringing the house down with it.

A decision was made. A great deception was undertaken. At the heart of the fraud was an accounting lie. Over the course of fifteen months, from 2001 to 2002, the company hid $3.8 billion in operating expenses, recording them in its books as "capital investments" and essentially counting the expenses as part of its cash flow. The accounting sleight of hand meant that WorldCom lost money over the fifteen-month period rather than earning more than $1.5 billion in profits, as it claimed to investors.

The Securities and Exchange Commission launched a wide-ranging investigation into the company in March 2002. The following month, Ebbers resigned as CEO. Two months later, the *New York Times* broke the news of the $3.8 billion fraud on its front page. The following month, the company filed for bankruptcy.[133]

At first, the company put the blame for the fraud on Scott Sullivan, WorldCom's chief financial officer. Eventually, a federal jury would decide that Ebbers, who maintained to the end that he was unaware of the fraud, was "a leader of criminal activity" at WorldCom. He was sentenced to twenty-five years in prison for securities fraud, conspiracy and filing false reports with regulators. He died in 2020, one month after being released due to his failing health.[134]

Investors, who had once believed in Ebbers, lost an estimated $175 billion on the company's implosion—a sum far greater than the combined losses of everyone who had been raided on the Mississippi River or robbed on the Trace. In the end, Ebbers could claim the dubious distinction of being the greatest bandit of all.[135]

Chapter 9

ACTS OF GOD

THE NEW MADRID EARTHQUAKES
AND THE TUPELO TORNADO OF 1936

THE NEW MADRID EARTHQUAKES

The earth is utterly broken, the earth is split apart, the earth is violently shaken.
—Isaiah 24:19

December 16, 1811

Nicholas Roosevelt stood serenely aboard the *New Orleans*. His feisty and supportive wife sat below with the happy couple's newborn son. On this day, the Roosevelts just might have been the most popular people in the country. The two—for Lydia refused to remain safely at home, despite being eight months pregnant—were taking the first trip on a steam-powered ship from Pittsburgh to the ship's namesake, the Crescent City. The *New Orleans* had already made it past the dangerous Falls of the Ohio; the rest of the trip would surely be smooth sailing.

The Roosevelts' Newfoundland dog, Tiger, walked up to Lydia and placed his head in her lap, whimpering. Something was wrong. Due to the immensity of the ship and the noise of the engine, the humans on board could not detect the reason for the dog's unease.

As the Roosevelts and their crew ate breakfast on a windless morning, they noticed trees swaying along the bank. And then, to their horror, they saw a large chunk of the riverbank crash into the river. Waves began to crash into, rock and lift the boat. Nausea and confusion and terror gripped those aboard. The captain steered the *New Orleans* into the middle of the river, hoping to avoid a plethora of fallen trees and sections of land that had collapsed along the sides. Captain Andrew Jack had sailed the Ohio and Mississippi Rivers many times before, but he was now on an unfamiliar river. Even familiar landmarks had disappeared. It quickly became clear to all that a massive earthquake had hit the western United States.[136]

The *New Orleans* pulled closer to the epicenter of the earthquake that afternoon: New Madrid, Missouri. Rather, they arrived at what *had been* New Madrid. The new town was a pile of ruins, fifteen feet lower than it had been on Captain Jack's last trip. Some of those on land fled from the strange house spitting steam on the river. Others begged to be taken aboard, far from New Madrid, far from the shaking earth. With limited provisions aboard, Roosevelt decided to continue down the river to New Orleans.[137]

Many others had decided that being on the Mississippi River was safer than being on land. For many, it would prove a fateful decision.

Late September 1811

Tecumseh had paid a visit to the southern nations—Choctaw, Chickasaw and Creek—in the hopes of uniting them with the northern Indian nations in a war to the death with the United States. His charisma and eloquence failed to move the overwhelming majority of his southern audience. He vented his frustration at the Creek leader Big Warrior: "You have taken my talk and the sticks and the wampum and the hatchet, but you do not mean to fight. I know the reason. You do not believe the Great Spirit has sent me. You shall know. I leave Tuckabatchee directly and shall go straight to Detroit. When I arrive there, I will stamp my foot on the ground and shake down every house in Tuckabatchee."[138] With that, Tecumseh returned north, taking few warriors with him and leaving behind only his prophecy.

THOSE ABOARD THE *NEW Orleans* had sailed in the direct path of what would come to be known as the New Madrid Earthquakes, the most powerful earthquakes to hit east of the Rocky Mountains. They were a series of three major quakes that occurred on December 16, 1811; January 23, 1812; and February 7, 1812. On the modern Richter scale, they would have measured between 7.2 and 8.1, 7.0 and 7.8 and 7.4 and 8.1, respectively.[139] To put it in perspective, the deadliest earthquake in U.S. history, the San Francisco quake of 1906 that killed more than three thousand people,

TECUMSEH.

Tecumseh. *Library of Congress.*

was a 7.9, and the famous "World Series" earthquake of 1989 was a 6.9. Jay Feldman explained, "Whatever the exact magnitudes may have been, one thing is undeniable—the December 16, January 23, and February 7 quakes were huge, and it was only the sparse population of the area and the wooden house construction that kept the death toll from reaching a catastrophic figure."[140]

The Mississippi River rose more than twenty feet and flowed backward. Eyewitnesses claimed that the earth had vomited, and large and deep crevices opened like the jaws of a beast, ready to devour those on land.[141]

The New Madrid earthquake and aftershocks were felt in Detroit (Lake Orchard began to bubble and boil); Charleston, South Carolina (the pavement cracked); New York City (cups and saucers rattled on tables); and Natchez, Mississippi (buildings began noticeably shaking).[142] The Natchez Trace, too, was forever altered by the phenomena. Much of the Trace would have experienced the following symptoms, according to the modified Mercalli Intensity scale: "[VI] Felt by all, many frightened and run outside. Some heavy furniture moved; a few instances of fallen plaster and damaged chimneys. Damage slight. [VII] Everybody runs outside. Damage negligible in buildings of good design and construction; slight to moderate damage in well-built ordinary structures; considerable damage in poorly built or badly designed structures; some chimneys broken."[143]

Because the Trace was sparsely populated, and war and treaties had forced the Indians living alongside it to leave in just a short while, there is no telling exactly how much damage occurred from Natchez to Nashville. There is, however, no doubt that those living along the path felt the earthquakes' rumbles.

THE PORTION OF ANDREW Jackson's troops who sailed to Natchez on his famous 1813 trek stopped in New Madrid and surveyed the extensive damage firsthand. They then boarded their boats and continued their trip to Natchez.

Not long after, Jackson's troops were marching up the Trace, home, toward Tennessee. The anxiety and stress of the march up the Trace, after the Wilkinson debacle, was heightened by the fear of an Indian attack. Jackson's soldiers, already exhausted and starving, marched in constant fear of ambush. After the New Madrid earthquakes, Indian attacks on settlers (mostly in the North, but with some notable and brutal examples near Nashville) had increased. Many Creek recalled Tecumseh's warning and took to the warpath. Jackson worried that the Chickasaw and Choctaw might cast their lot with the Red Creek[144] and join Tecumseh's movement.

Fortunately for Jackson and his men, the Choctaw and Chickasaw remained loyal to the United States and provided lifesaving assistance on the Volunteers' homeward trek. The earthquake did, however, unite the northern nations, and a savage war broke out in the Detroit region, culminating in the death of Tecumseh, another massive Indian removal and the future election of two U.S. presidents.[145]

December 30, 1812

The passengers aboard the *New Orleans* saw Natchez in the distance. The steamboat proudly sailed toward the city on the bluffs. But then the engine went out, and it drifted past the city, out of control. However, Captain Jack was able to get the steam up, and the paddle wheel began to move the boat against the current, amazing the residents of Natchez. Twelve days later, it was in New Orleans, the voyage complete. Despite all the prognostications of doom, the Roosevelts, their crew and the *New Orleans* proved that a steamboat could indeed make the arduous trip down the Mississippi River. And it did so during one of the most destructive natural events in the young nation's history.[146]

Sixty other boats, with an unknown number of passengers, were caught on the river during the earthquakes. Their crews now rest in a watery grave in the Father of Waters.

THE TUPELO TORNADO, 1936

I would hurry to my place of shelter, far from the tempest and storm.
—*Psalm 55:8*

Palm Sunday

Jim Burrough looked at the sky from his house on Highway 6, on the western edge of Tupelo, Mississippi. He did not like what he saw in the sky. It had been a warm and humid evening, with a breeze in the air. Around 7:30 p.m., it began to rain, and the sky darkened by the minute. Then he saw the ominous storm clouds…and the funnel.

Vernon and Gladys had just moved into the home he built for their expanding family on 306 Old Saltillo Drive in East Tupelo. Vernon had borrowed $180 to build that house. Less than a year later, Gladys gave birth to twins, but only one survived. Now the parents were recovering from their loss and enjoying their fifteen-month-old boy.[147] They, too, saw the storm clouds approaching on this sultry evening.

AT 8:17 P.M. ON April 5, one of the deadliest tornadoes in U.S. history descended on Tupelo, Mississippi. There was little warning when the F5[148] twister landed to the west of the city. It destroyed lives and property as it made its way to the heart of Tupelo. An eyewitness survivor later recalled:

That cloud, or funnel, traveled fast, and although it was quite dark, I could see big objects lifted off the ground and sent whirling upward and around. It was a terrible thing to watch. It struck Tupelo squarely in the middle....

Well, it tore into the houses in the western part of the city and shattered them like they were bits of kindling or piles of leaves. Wreckage and debris was flying around in the air....Every house it touched seemed to crumble and collapse into a pile of jagged and splintered lumber.

I heard people shouting and screaming. I heard groans and cries that wrenched the heart. But those inside the house outside the storm's path couldn't very well get out until the winds died down. No man could have stood on his feet in that storm.

The racket was simply deafening.[149]

The tornado tore through Willis Heights, the wealthy section of town, and leveled a number of mansions, and then it proceeded to the residential area and the African American section—"Shake Rag" and "On the Hill." Many residents were blown into Gum Pond, which would be dredged over the next few days, uncovering dozens of bodies. The tornado was an equal-opportunity destroyer in 1936 Jim Crow Mississippi. All of Tupelo felt the brunt of its wrath. The *Coffeeville Courier* reported:

Trees were uprooted, driven through houses. Chimneys crashed. Porches were carried away. Trucks and automobiles spun drunkenly across deserted streets. Beds were catapulted through windows with their sleeping victims tangled in the covers. Roofs crashed on scores who prayed in howling

darkness. This kept up for 15 minutes. Then fire broke out. Rain fell and
the night was filled with screams and groans of the injured.
"It was a nightmare out of hell," a witness said soberly.[150]

When the three-block-wide, three-hundred-mile-per-hour storm passed less than twenty minutes later, Tupelo looked like a war zone. More than one thousand homes were destroyed or severely damaged. At least 216 people were dead or at the point of death, with another 700 injured. Pine needles were driven into tree trunks, and chickens were found dead, completely stripped of their feathers.[151] It was the fourth-deadliest tornado in U.S. history.[152]

The Tupelo hospital was damaged, and so emergency hospitals, triage centers and morgues were set up wherever possible—churches, still-standing houses, the Lyric movie theater and more. The county courthouse also took in the dying and wounded. Captain C.E. Lehmberg was placed in charge and told reporters:

> *We have no estimate of the number of those now being treated for injuries. They are being brought in by the dozens every ten minutes, and many of the number are dying soon after arriving here. We sent about one hundred injured to Memphis this morning on a special train, but I do not believe more than sixty percent of those on the train will reach Memphis alive.*[153]

Tupelo was in the dark, with no phone service. Sporadic fires began to spring up throughout the city because of downed powerlines. The water tower, too, was blown down, so there was no water to extinguish the fires. Fortunately, it began to rain again, and the fires were doused. Eventually, word of the catastrophe got out. Help began to pour into the little town in the form of the CCC, Red Cross, National Guard and American Legion. The Tennessee Valley Authority sent workers to restore electricity.[154] The City of Memphis sent doctors and nurses and ran trains back and forth, bringing the wounded to their own hospital.

With the phone lines down, concerned family members could not get through. Even those in Tupelo had to rely on the daily lists of the dead and wounded run in the newspaper to locate their loved ones. And those lists grew as each day passed. Many of those who could still walk searched the town, going through makeshift morgues and looking under sheets for friends and family. Bodies were brought in on trucks and wagons from the country. "Through the main streets of the town they drove, looking for a place in an empty store, the courthouse, city hall, or just anywhere in seclusion where they might deposit the bodies of victims."[155]

The number of victims recovered from the wreckage, from the lake and from the fields continued to grow.

JIM BURROUGH WAS FOUND in the wreckage of his house. He was alive and conscious. His rescuers carried him to the courthouse, hoping to get him lifesaving care. As Jim waited there, the search and rescue team began to bring in the other members of his immediate family—his wife and children—by ones and two: Jennie, Allen, Carl, Doris, Dorothy, George, Inez, James, John, Sarah, Thomas and Vonceile. They had been found scattered around the neighboring field. Only his wife, Jennie, sixteen-year-old John Walter and baby Allen were still alive. The rest were corpses, the first victims of the deadly tornado. Within hours, the other three died as well. Father Jim followed the other dozen members of his family, conscious until the moment he, too, passed on.

The thirteen Burroughs were buried in a single grave, seven feet wide and thirty feet long. There was a shortage of coffins; most were buried in plain pine boxes. Yet family, friends and acquaintances made sure that when all was said and done, each Burrough was buried in his or her own coffin. Five hundred persons showed up for the last rites. It was a rushed funeral on account of the sheer numbers awaiting burial and the fact that there were only so many ministers to go around.

With the rites concluded, the participants walked away singing "In the Sweet By and By" (quietly so as not to disturb the nearby funerals taking place).[156]

> *In the sweet by and by,*
> *We shall meet on that beautiful shore.*
> *We shall sing on that beautiful shore*
> *The melodious songs of the blessed;*
> *And our spirits shall sorrow no more,*
> *Not a sigh for the blessing of rest.*[157]

The tornado bypassed Gladys and Vernon's house. The impoverished couple who lived on welfare, who needed charity to pay the fifteen-dollar doctor bill to birth their beloved son and who relied on neighbors and friends for diapers were fortunate to have the tornado bypass their humble home. The

First house of Elvis Presley. *Ryan Starrett.*

struggling trio survived the Tupelo tornado of 1936. Tupelo resident Mem Leake later explained, "I think it was more capriciousness than anything else. You can't explain why one house is here and the one next to it is not."[158]

Fortunately for Tupelo—and music aficionados everywhere—the infant and his parents survived. The three spent the next dozen years moving from house to house, job to job, along Tupelo and the Natchez Trace,[159] before finally relocating to Memphis, Tennessee.

When he was ten years old, Gladys and Vernon's little child would perform "Old Shep" at the Mississippi-Alabama Fair and Dairy Show.[160] Years later, he would be performing "Blue Suede Shoes," "In the Ghetto" and "Hound Dog" to crowds of thousands, adored by millions and on his way to becoming an American icon.

Elvis Presley was one of the fortunate ones who survived the Tupelo tornado of 1936.

Chapter 10

"WAGON LOADS OF PIGEONS"

A SPECTACULAR BIRD VANISHES FROM THE TRACE

Night of Slaughter

On the morning of September 23, 1831, readers of the *Vicksburg Whig* opened their papers to find a detailed and horrific account of animal slaughter. The narrative was written by the naturalist, painter and erstwhile resident of Natchez John James Audubon. In his narrative, Audubon described a scene unimaginable to modern Americans.

He had ridden forty miles through a broad swath of forest to reach the site he described. It was a pigeon roost—a section of woods that innumerable migrating passenger pigeons had chosen to use as a stopping point. Audubon knew when he had reached the roost because the area looked like it had been hit by a tornado. Tree limbs had been snapped off, whole trees were broken down to jagged spikes and the ground was covered by an inches-thick layer of droppings. When he arrived in the afternoon, there were no birds—at least, no living birds. But there were dozens of people, waiting around the roost with guns, poles, pine-knot torches, horses, wagons and pots of sulfur. And there were three hundred pigs, driven to the spot by two farmers.

Around sundown, the pigeons began to arrive, creating their own wind and a cacophony that drowned out all other sounds. The gathered people started shooting (Audubon wrote that he could not even hear the gunshots amid the noise of the birds) and swatting at the birds with poles. Thousands of birds fell immediately. The birds did not stop arriving at the spot until

John James Audubon.
National Portrait Gallery.

midnight. They piled on top of tree branches and even themselves, creating heavy balls of feathers and flesh. The weight of the birds broke many branches, and groups of birds were crushed by the falling debris. All the while, people continued to kill.

Those who did not kill plucked and salted the dead birds, discarding what was left in large piles. The farmers released their pigs into the scene of carnage, and the animals ate the birds that lay on the ground.

Audubon could not quantify the number of pigeons that had come to the spot that night, only saying that it was "beyond conception." He spent the entire night observing the slaughter by firelight, unable to speak to anyone else because of the noise. When morning came, the pigeons that had survived flew away, resuming their migration. As the pigeons departed, the other animals of the forest arrived to feast on what was left behind. Audubon recorded seeing bears, foxes, lynxes, cougars, raccoons, 'possums, ferrets, eagles, hawks and, of course, vultures. And when the pigeons had left, taking their cacophony with them, another sound hung in the air: the howling of wolves.[161]

That night, Audubon became one of the last humans to witness the migration of the passenger pigeon, a phenomenon that had been occurring for one million years before humans ever reached North America. When white Americans began moving into the interior of the continent, it is estimated that passenger pigeons made up between 25 and 40 percent of all birds in North America. There were more passenger pigeons alive than any other bird. But within one human generation, the species would disappear from the earth.[162]

Passenger Pigeons on the Natchez Trace

Nathaniel Folsom's foot first touched Choctaw soil around 1775. He was nineteen and already a sixth-generation American. Folsom had left his birthplace of North Carolina, carried along with his mother and siblings to the Choctaw village of Bok Tuklo by his father. His father wanted to live in the Indian country, where "money grew on bushes."

Shortly after arriving at Bok Tuklo, Folsom and his father quarreled. His father knocked him down, and Folsom walked away, effectively emancipating himself. His parents left him there, moving north to the Chickasaw Nation. Folsom was barely an adult but found himself alone in a foreign land. He became the apprentice to "Welch," another man living in Bok Tuklo. Welch taught him how to trade in the Indian country.[163]

Folsom became a successful trader, marrying two high-status Choctaw women and fathering twenty-four children between them—including a future chief of the Choctaw Nation. As travel on the Natchez Trace increased around the end of the eighteenth century, Folsom saw an opportunity; he would move from Bok Tuklo to a spot on the Natchez Trace, where he would establish the first substantial stand along the Choctaw stretch of the road.[164]

He chose an auspicious site for his stand. It would sit beside a place similar to what Audubon would go on to describe thirty years later: a six-hundred-acre swath of forest used as a roost by migrating passenger pigeons. A small creek ran through the area and watered the migrating birds; settlers called it "Pigeon Roost Creek." Folsom's stand, located near present-day Mathiston, Mississippi, would be called "Folsom's Pigeon Roost." He had not found the place where money grew on bushes, but he had found a spot that would provide an enormous quantity of delectable meat a few times a year.

John James Audubon's painting of the passenger pigeon. *Audubon.org.*

The bird that lent its name to Folsom's stand was similar to the mourning dove—a bird still plentiful in Mississippi today. But it was larger and behaved very differently. A writer in the early twentieth century described the passenger pigeon as "beautiful, grayish-brown birds with the iridescent golden sheen upon their throats."[165] Unlike the mourning dove, or any other bird alive then, the passenger pigeon traveled in groups of up to 2 billion, eating enormous quantities of acorns, chestnuts, beechnuts, seeds and berries as they traveled across eastern North America.

Their appetites were so large that they would out-compete wild turkeys, leaving them lean and emaciated. Although they wintered in Mississippi and the other southern states, they nested in the northern states and Canada. Trees would sometimes hold one hundred nests apiece. The birds traveled and nested in such large flocks as a means of defense from predators, and their breeding behavior depended on large colonies. Their gregarious nature would one day become a key vulnerability.[166]

A reverend traveling along the Natchez Trace around 1806 described what was very likely the pigeon roost that gave Folsom's stand its name. While traveling through a swamp, he stopped along the road to observe the roost, which he described as so "marvellous" that he wouldn't have even told anyone about it if there were not other witnesses there to verify he was telling the truth. The whole mile-wide section of forest looked like it had been struck by a hurricane. Pigeons sat on every tree, bending the smallest over so that their foliage looked like brooms hanging upside down. He described a hickory tree a foot in diameter that had doubled over under the weight of the birds; its top was touching the ground, and its roots had emerged from the soil, creating a ridge. Underneath every tree lay a pile of pigeon droppings—enough droppings to fill thousands of wagons, the reverend estimated.[167]

At the time Europeans began moving to the Choctaw Nation, the Choctaw used the vicinity of the Trace for hunting grounds rather than for settlement. The Choctaw were semi-agricultural, supplementing their crops with a variety of game, including the passenger pigeon. The Choctaw would range widely to exploit hunting opportunities, and Folsom's Pigeon Roost represented a conspicuous, reliable and rich opportunity.

Early travelers recorded that the pigeon was a key avian prey species for southeastern Indians, usually second to turkeys. One witness wrote in the 1730s that Indians in Carolina used the passenger pigeon not only as a meat source but also as a source of oil. In years when the passenger pigeon hunt was particularly successful, Indians would preserve the pigeons' fat and use it to supplement their diets throughout the winter, spreading the fat on bread. Another man traveling through the South in the 1840s described hunting (or rather collecting) passenger pigeons with an Indian group. At the site of the roost, the ground was covered with dead and dying pigeons that had fallen from broken branches. The Indians loaded their horses with as many pigeons as they could carry, and their dogs had "gone mad with feeding on their putrefied remains."[168]

Although humans had been preying on passenger pigeons for ten thousand years, human predation did not seem to have a noticeable impact on their population sizes until commercial hunting began in the nineteenth century, facilitated by the clear-cutting of eastern forests and the construction of railroads and canals. The birds had fewer places to nest, and hunters could reach those nesting sites and transport their salted meat more easily. At one nesting site in Michigan, hunters killed fifty thousand birds a day for five straight months. Much of the meat went to New York City, where pigeons were sold on the market for as little as fifty cents per dozen.[169]

When Folsom established his stand sometime around 1801, the passenger pigeon slaughter had not yet begun in earnest. In 1835, a writer in Columbus, Mississippi, made reference to the flocks of pigeons that still filled the forest. By the 1880s, so many of the birds had been killed that hunters could no longer reliably bring them to market.[170]

By 1911, Mississippi newspapers were printing stories about the last living passenger pigeon, a female living at a zoo in Cincinnati. Papers printed stories about a university offering a reward of $1,500 to anyone who could locate a passenger pigeon nest. No one ever claimed the reward.[171]

A *Clarion Ledger* story about Folsom's stand, published in 1947, less than three decades after the extinction of the passenger pigeon, attempted to absolve Mississippians of any part in the passenger pigeon slaughter. Pigeon hunting had been a great pastime at Folsom's stand, the author wrote, but neither local hunters nor farmers participated in the "wholesale slaughter" perpetuated in the northern states. It was the northern hunters' "greed and sometimes wanton sport" that caused the destruction of the species. But other stories, passed down through generations, tell of Mississippians who visited Pigeon Roost Creek during the migration and left with wagons full of the birds, "whose numbers seemed to be almost infinite."[172]

Revelations

The passenger pigeon instantly became a warning of what terrible ecological damage humans can wreak if unchecked. But the true story of the passenger pigeon's demise was not fully understood for another one hundred years.

In the late twentieth century, archaeologists were confronted with a puzzle regarding the species: the bones of the birds were rather uncommon in prehistoric Indian middens. If the passenger pigeon was such a ubiquitous species, more evidence of its exploitation by hunters should exist in the archaeological record. Archaeologists hypothesized that maybe the bird had not always existed in such abundance in North America.

A few decades later, archaeologists' suspicions were confirmed by geneticists. Using samples of passenger pigeon DNA, a Taiwanese team of researchers discovered that the historical population of the passenger pigeon was about 1/10,000[th] of what existed when Audubon observed the birds in the 1800s. The passenger pigeon population fluctuated widely based on food availability, and the arrival of humans to North America coincided with a massive explosion in the passenger pigeon population (settlers may have even contributed to the population explosion by planting crops and removing competition for food resources by Indians). The passenger pigeon population was naturally bound to crash, but when it began to, human exploitation of its nesting and roosting sites drove its population to a terminally low number. Humans certainly caused the extinction of the species, but the complete picture was somewhat more complicated.[173]

For centuries, Indians and settlers had welcomed the migration of what the Seneca called *jah'gowa*, or "big bread." It was a spectacle of abundance that humans thought would never end. From now on, though, Americans will only know the passenger pigeon by a painting left to us by John James Audubon. In the painting, a mother pigeon, her feathers colored blue, cream and peach, passes nuts from her mouth into the mouth of her baby. It is a depiction of continuance that was painted, sadly, in the species's final days.

Chapter 11

A FIERY END

THE TRAGIC TALES OF DANIEL BURNETT AND SAM BURNS

Who among us can dwell with the consuming fire?
Who among us can dwell with everlasting burnings?
—Isaiah 33:14

DANIEL BURNETT

Colonel Daniel Burnett was the American dream. He followed in the footsteps of his heroic father (a soldier of the Revolution who served under the famed Swamp Fox, Francis Marion) and lived a life of adventure and public service. When still young, he moved down the Natchez Trace and established a stand at Grindstone Ford on the Bayou Pierre River. It was the line between civilization (the Natchez district) and the wilderness (the Trace running northeast). But Burnett was the type of man who thrived in both worlds. He befriended the Choctaw, fought for Spain in Spanish Texas and later for the Americans in the War of 1812. He was tough enough, charismatic enough and respected enough to be elected to the Mississippi Territorial House of Representatives. Shortly after, he was one of the forty-five framers of Mississippi's first constitution.[174]

In 1821, Daniel Burnett had it all: respect, money, political prestige and more. More prestigious positions awaited him as he entered the winter of his life. And then his grandsons—given to him by his only child, Jane—would carry on his legacy. But it all went up in flames during a warm June evening.

June 25, 1821

Jane Patterson sent her oldest boy upstairs to retrieve some spirits from a barrel. Eleven-year-old John did his mother's bidding and ascended the steps. His six-year-old brother, Jarrett, followed him. As John poured the alcohol, a curious Jarrett held a candle to the spout. The explosion was immediate. Both boys were hurled back, aflame. The roof caught fire, and the upstairs furniture was immediately ablaze.

John and Jarrett were dragged from the house and treated in the yard, but it was too late. Their burns were fatal. Weeping and in agony, they told what had happened upstairs. Within hours, both boys were dead.

Gravestone of Daniel Burnett at Grindstone Ford. *Ryan Starrett.*

Less than two months later, their distraught father was buried beside his boys. Two weeks shy of the anniversary of little John and Jarrett's death, their sickly mother followed. All four Pattersons were buried near the ruins of their home at Grindstone Ford.[175]

Daniel Burnett—colonel, representative, senator, Speaker of the House and bereaved father and grandfather—was heartbroken. He went on to serve his community and state for another half decade before dying at age sixty-three. He was buried at Grindstone Ford Cemetery, next to his daughter, son-in-law and two grandchildren.[176]

SAM BURNS

March 14, 1908

Twenty-one-year-old Sam Burns was a hardworking, respected citizen of Natchez. He was a trained plumber who had the full confidence of his employer. A member of the volunteer fire department and city guard, Burns was an active and fruitful member of his community.

Burns was working at a house on North Pearl Street when he received an urgent message to get to the four-story Natchez Drug Company building. Employees had smelled gas. Burns himself had recently placed a gas stove on the fourth floor where the chemists worked. Sensing potential danger, Burns promptly made his way to the corner of Main Street and Union. He did what he was trained to do when there was a suspected gas leak: he lit a candle and walked along the pipes. If there was a leak, the area around would flare up. Burns would then patch it up and return to his job on North Pearl Street.

Only, there was no leak on the fourth floor. "The leak is not here; it must be somewhere below." When he got to the first floor, he found the leak.[177]

The following day, the headline for the *Daily Democrat* read:

Life and Property Lost in Flames
Eight Buried Under Brick and Iron

Terrific Explosion in Laboratory of Natchez Drug Company Sends Chemist and Seven Girls Into Eternity—Falling Walls Crush Adjoining Building Injuring John Carkeet—Carpenter Jumped From Third Story Breaking His Neck—Sparks From Blazing Ruins Sends Fire to Eighteen Residences—City Under Martial Law—Relief Work Will Begin This Morning—Loss Estimated at $200,000 Almost Covered by Insurance—Sam Burns Has Been Reported Among the Missing—Inquest Today

The resulting explosion destroyed the five-story building housing the Natchez Drug Company as well as two other downtown buildings. Several residences were set aflame, but a resourceful fire department saved most of the area. Nevertheless, Natchez was placed under martial law for several days as volunteers attempted to recover the missing bodies inside—and to keep overzealous Samaritans a safe distance from the still smoldering building.

Eventually, all the deceased were recovered to the relief—and horror—of the community.

Cleveland Laub was a twenty-two-year-old chemist in charge of the laboratory. On that fateful day, he heard the explosion, knew it was the gas leak and saw the walls tumbling in around him. He was trapped. With the flames roaring around him, he covered himself with a mattress to protect himself from debris and fire. His body was found the next day, charred, covered by debris and still beneath the mattress.

Uriah Hoskins was a carpenter working on the third story of the doomed building. When the explosion erupted, he was blown out the window to the pavement below.[178] Two witnesses saw him arise, stagger about and collapse again. They promptly moved him across the street to the cathedral grounds, where he died. His neck was broken and skull cracked.

John Carkeet, Confederate veteran of the Natchez Rifles as well as the Siege of Jackson, the Battle of Chickamauga and Atlanta Campaign, was standing outside his home conversing with a friend when several pieces of debris pierced his legs between his ankles and knees. The well-respected war hero and undertaker of Natchez died in his bed two days later.

Six female employees—one married and five single—were killed in the explosion. The five single girls were ages twelve to twenty-two, and none of them was from Natchez. They had come specifically to make their way in the world by working for the company.

Willie Kates was a fifteen-year-old Black porter. His body was found alongside Inez Netterville on the north end of the building shortly after midnight. His dead body was pulled from the debris and handed over for burial.

RUMORS BEGAN TO SPREAD that Burns was the culprit—and deliberately so. Some claimed to have seen him about town after the explosion. Yet those rumors were put to rest when his charred body was recovered two days later, six feet from the pipe he had been investigating. The force of the explosion had immediately blown him back, and then the collapsing building deposited his body on the basement floor. He was recognized only by his suspenders and his ring. Unable to get the body in a sheet, Burns's friends had to scoop up the body as gently as possible and place it immediately in a coffin.

Burns's corpse was taken to the fire department to await burial, but only after a posthumous inquest was held to determine his guilt.

JOHN CHAMBLISS, OWNER OF the Natchez Drug Company, placed an ad in the following day's paper:

> We are now, and since the moment of the conflagration, have been under a mental and physical strain, almost beyond endurance, but we hope to survive to reestablish ourselves, for we are not among the class of "quitters," nor of those that doubt the future of Natchez and surrounding territory.

Chambliss also built a lasting and iconic monument to the five single women/girls who lost their lives preparing the medicinal concoctions that alleviated so much suffering in Natchez:[179]

Turning Angel, Natchez City Cemetery. *Ryan Starrett.*

ERECTED BY THE NATCHEZ DRUG COMPANY TO THE MEMORY OF THE UNFORTUNATE EMPLOYEES WHO LOST THEIR LIVES IN THE GREAT DISASTER THAT DESTROYED ITS BUILDING ON MARCH 14, 1908.

CARRIE D MURRAY
INEZ NETTERVILLE
LUELLA D BOOTH
MARY E WORTHY
ADA WHITE

The five women were buried beneath the gaze of what quickly became known as the "Turning Angel," whose eyes allegedly follow travelers as they pass up and down Cemetery Road. Their monument has become synonymous with Natchez. Willie Kates got no such memorial.[180]

THREE DAYS AFTER THE explosion, Sam Burns was exonerated. The court determined that he was only doing his job in the way that he had been trained. In fact, Sam Burns was an honorable man and an unfortunate victim. The local paper reported the court's findings:

[Y]*oung Burns, the youth who gave his life with the others would have sacrificed all that he held dear before doing as he did, if he could have but known, no man knowing him would undertake to question for a moment. That he employed the same method that has been the practise for years and years by old and experienced men and is known to all plumbers and to many who are not.*

Let no man forget that poor Sam Burns was a volunteer fireman and a member of one of our military companies, ready at all times to serve his people, placing life and limb in jeopardy without hesitation....

A higher hand than that of man directed his movements in that fatal hour and all should feel thankful that the last chapter in this awful tragedy has been written.

Sam Burns was granted a burial with full honors as the community quickly forgave and mourned one of its cherished sons.[181]

Chapter 12

TO BE OR NOT TO BE?

THAT WAS THE QUESTION FOR MERIWETHER LEWIS, NAOMI JUDD AND BRIANA BROWNE

*Suicide is not a blot on anyone's name; it is a tragedy....
[I]n the end, for all of us, it is his life that remains.*
—*Kay Jamison*[182]

MERIWETHER LEWIS

October 11, 1809

The most recognizable hero in the United States, the governor of the Upper Louisiana Territory and the protégé of Thomas Jefferson put a pistol to his head and blew off the uppermost part of his skull. He reached for a second pistol, shoved it into his abdomen and fired again. Disappointed at still being alive, he crawled along the floor, climbed into bed and began slashing himself with a razor blade.

When a servant entered his room the following morning, the man in the bed asked for water and begged that the servant finish the job. He gasped, "I am no coward; but I am so strong, so hard to die." Not long after, Meriwether Lewis drew his last breath, a victim of his own hand—and so much more.[183]

Meriwether Lewis died on October 11, 1809, at Grinder's Stand along the Natchez Trace.[184] His descent into a suicidal abyss began three years before, when he returned home as the leader of the Corps of Discovery, having made an eight-thousand-mile journey across the North American

Meriwether Lewis. *National Portrait Gallery.*

continent to the Pacific Ocean. The odyssey, which still ranks among the most important and impressive explorations ever by an U.S. citizen, brought him instant fame and turned him into a living legend. When he returned east, he was wined and dined and feted wherever he went. After three years journeying to the Pacific Ocean and back, Lewis's future was as bright as any man's. His good friend President Jefferson rewarded him with the position as governor of the Upper Louisiana Territory. He was commissioned to write what would certainly be an immediate bestseller and one of the most important books of the century: the tale of the Corps of Discovery. He had everything a man could dream of. His connection to his friend and patron Thomas Jefferson made even the presidency of the United States of America a future possibility.

August 18, 1805

On his thirty-first birthday, Meriwether Lewis sat in the wide-open West. The Corps of Discovery was at a crossroads. His friend and partner, William Clark, left that morning to search for the headwaters of the Columbia River. Lewis prepared to descend into the valley where Sacagawea's Shoshone lived. He was already where no U.S. citizen had been before. But it wasn't enough for Lewis. His brilliant, active mind, capable at once of mastering logistics and of profound introspection, reflected on the day and his life:

> *This day I completed my thirty first year, and conceived that I had in all human probability now existed about half the period which I am to remain in this sublunary world. I reflected that I had done but little, very little indeed, to further the happiness of the human race, or to advance the information of the succeeding generation. I viewed with regret the many hours I have spent in indolence, and now soarly feel the want of that information which those hours would have given me had they been judiciously expended.*[185]

Lewis shut his journal and began to prepare for the following day.

March 1807–June 1809

After a yearlong delay in Philadelphia, where once again he was honored wherever he went and where he made numerous arrangements with scientists and artists to assist with his great book, Lewis finally headed to St. Louis to assume his duties as governor.

The tedium of the position disappointed Lewis. He began to suffer what psychologists call the "Buzz Aldrin Syndrome." Lewis had been to the proverbial moon. He had seen wonders and undergone experiences incomprehensible to the rank and file. And now he sat behind a desk in St. Louis, filing papers. Although it was always lurking, sometimes manifesting itself but most often under control when his mind and body were so actively engaged on his great odyssey, depression began to take control of Lewis's mind.

In addition to the drudgery of being governor, Lewis was constantly ridiculed and undermined by his territorial secretary, Frederick Bates. Bates had acted as governor during Lewis's long delay in getting to St. Louis. During that time, he had built up his own personal power base, and he intended to remove the interim title. As soon as Lewis arrived, Bates unleashed a flood of letters to Washington condemning Jefferson's appointment.

In 1808, there was a new president, James Madison, and he didn't feel the same responsibility to Lewis as had his predecessor.

June–August 1809

The tedium and the backstabbing wore on the new governor. He managed as best he could, but then there was that other project hanging over his head: his literary magnus opus—the account of their expedition in book form. Much was expected of Lewis. The public awaited his tome.

But Lewis was a chronic procrastinator—as evidenced by it taking a full year for him to travel from Washington to St. Louis to resume his gubernatorial duties. He also may have doubted his ability to write. So, he put it off. Month after month. Year after year. Soon, even Jefferson became irritated at the delay. He wrote letters to Lewis, wondering why the governor had ceased corresponding with him. He asked about the progress of the book. Lewis made no answer to his patron, his father figure, the president of the United States. Jefferson, one of the great minds of his age, had hyped up the book and spoken to many of its importance, and he was impatient for its publication. But Lewis had no answer—there was no book.

Clay Jenkinson explained, "The West was mightier than the pen—at least his pen. He could not write prose equal to his own expectations."[186] So, Lewis pushed the book into the back of his mind and sought solace elsewhere.

August 1809

Meriwether Lewis received an unwelcome letter from Secretary of War William Eustis. The U.S. government was rejecting a number of Lewis's invoices. The governor had taken on several debts in his role as territorial governor expecting to be reimbursed. Now that recompense would not be forthcoming, placing Lewis in a financial bind. He also saw it as a personal condemnation. His competency—and his honor—was being questioned by the Madison administration. On August 18, he fired off an angry letter to Eustis: "Be assured Sir, that my country can never make 'A Burr' of me—She may reduce me to Poverty; but she can never sever my Attachment from her."[187]

Bored, depressed and now dishonored, Lewis determined to go to Washington and personally defend his character. Upon hearing that his political enemy, James Wilkinson, was sailing up the Mississippi River, Lewis decided against sailing to New Orleans and then up the Atlantic. Instead, he would disembark at Chickasaw Bluffs, connect with the Natchez Trace and proceed to Nashville.[188]

September 11–15, 1809

Lewis went ashore at New Madrid and made his will. His mother was his sole beneficiary. Four days later, he disembarked at Chickasaw Bluffs[189] and wrote a second will, making his friend William Clark the executor. He also wrote a personal letter to Clark in which he handed over much of his property to pay his debts. Clark immediately became worried over his friend's state of mind. Two months later, Clark read of his good friend's death in a newspaper. He wrote to his confidant and brother, Jonathan Clark:

> *I saw in a Frankfurt paper called the Arguss a report published which gives me much Concern, it Says that Govr. Lewis killed himself by Cutting his Throat with a Knife, on his way between the Chickasaw Bluffs and nashville, I fear this report has too much truth.... [M]y reasons for thinking it possible is founded on the letter which I recved from him at your house.... O! I fear the waight of his mind has overcome him.*[190]

When the fort's commander, Gilbert Russell, learned from the boat's crew that Lewis had tried to kill himself twice since leaving St. Louis, and when he saw that Lewis was not well,[191] he took him in. Russell would later relate to President Jefferson:

His untimely death may be attributed Solely to the free use he made of liquor which he acknowledged very candidly to me after he recovered & expressed a firm determination never to drink any more Spirits or use Snuff again both of which I deprived him of for Several days & confined him to Claret & a little white wine.

The truth was that Lewis had been drinking excessively for a while. So much so that Jefferson was already aware of "the habit into which he had fallen."[192]

Lewis remained clean for two weeks as he recovered at Chickasaw Bluffs. But whatever malady afflicted him, in addition to his alcoholism, returned as he made his way toward and then up the Natchez Trace. He had left Chickasaw Bluffs in the company of the local Indian agent, James Neelly. Russell would later explain:

But after leaving this place by some means or other his resolution left him and this agt. [Neelly] being extremely fond of liquor, instead of preventing the Govr. from drinking or putting him under any restraint, advised him to it & from everything I can learn gave the man every chance to seek an opportunity to destroy himself.

October 10–11, 1809

Whatever torment he was enduring—a chronic illness, withdrawals or the very nadir of depression—Lewis arrived at Grinder's Stand on the evening of October 10 in an agitated state. The day before, several horses had run away, and so Neelly stayed behind to search for them.[193] Lewis arrived with his servants, who were promptly housed away from the inn.

Priscilla Grinder, whose husband was away at the time, later reported that Lewis was walking back and forth across the inn, talking to himself in an agitated way, frightening Grinder. But then

he lighted his pipe, and drawing a chair to the door sat down, saying to Mrs. Grinder, in a kind tone of voice, "Madam this is a very pleasant evening." He smoked for some time, but quitted his seat and traversed the yard as before. He again sat down to his pipe, seemed again composed, and casting his eyes wishfully towards the west, observed what a sweet evening it was. Mrs. Grinder was preparing a bed for him; but he said he would sleep on the floor, and desired the servant to bring the bear skins and buffalo robe, which were immediately spread out for him.[194]

Above: Grinder's Stand, the site of Meriwether Lewis's death, milepost 385.9. *Ryan Starrett.*

Right: Meriwether Lewis's tomb. The top is unfinished to mark a life cut short before it was finished. *Ryan Starrett.*

Above: Tomb of Meriwether Lewis. *Ryan Starrett.*

Opposite: Memorial near Grinder's Stand, the site of Lewis's death. *Ryan Starrett.*

MERIWETHER LEWIS
1774-1809.

BENEATH THIS MONUMENT ERECTED UNDER LEGISLATIVE ACT BY THE STATE OF TENNESSEE, A.D. 1848, REPOSES THE DUST OF MERIWETHER LEWIS, A CAPTAIN IN THE UNITED STATES ARMY, PRIVATE SECRETARY TO PRESIDENT JEFFERSON, SENIOR COMMANDER OF THE LEWIS AND CLARK EXPEDITION, AND GOVERNOR OF THE TERRITORY OF LOUISIANA.

IN THE GRINDER HOUSE, THE RUINS OF WHICH ARE STILL DISCERNIBLE, 230 YARDS SOUTH OF THIS SPOT, HIS LIFE OF ROMANTIC ENDEAVOR AND LASTING ACHIEVEMENT CAME TRAGICALLY AND MYSTERIOUSLY TO ITS CLOSE ON THE NIGHT OF OCT. 11, 1809.

THE REPORT OF THE COMMITTEE APPOINTED TO CARRY OUT THE PROVISIONS OF THE MONUMENT ACT, CONTAINS THESE SIGNIFICANT STATEMENTS: "GREAT CARE WAS TAKEN TO IDENTIFY THE GRAVE. GEORGE NIXON, ESQ., AN OLD SURVEYOR, HAD BECOME VERY EARLY ACQUAINTED WITH THE LOCALITY. HE POINTED OUT THE PLACE; BUT TO MAKE ASSURANCE DOUBLY SURE THE GRAVE WAS RE-OPENED AND THE UPPER PORTION OF THE SKELETON EXAMINED AND SUCH EVIDENCE FOUND AS TO LEAVE NO DOUBT OF THE PLACE OF INTERMENT."

Once things quieted down and everyone retired, in the midst of a moonless night, Priscilla heard two gunshots from the cabin. Terrified—of Lewis's behavior just hours before and of bandits that still made the Trace a dangerous place—Grinder remained behind in her servants' cabin with her children. In the morning, Lewis was found in his room, breathing his final breaths.

His friend and father figure, Thomas Jefferson, with understanding and pity, summed up the death of one of America's greatest heroes: "About 3 oclock in the night he did the deed which plunged his friends into affliction and deprived his country of one of her most valued citizens."[195]

NAOMI JUDD

Naomi Judd drove onto the Natchez Trace Bridge. A few minutes later, she drove her car back off the bridge. She had made a last-second decision to live—at least for another day. And then another. And another. Years later, Judd would write:

> *I knew exactly how I was going to carry out my suicide. I wouldn't park at one end of the bridge, where people might stop me or question what I was*

doing. I would drive my car to the very center, the highest point, and in one swift motion open the car door and climb over the railing. After the 155-foot drop to State Route 96 below, it would all be over, now and forever. I would be out of this relentless torment.[196]

Despite her financial success and popularity, Judd was in the midst of despair, a dark night of the soul. After finishing a tour with her sister, she returned home to Kentucky, where she spent weeks hiding in her house, resisting attempts by her husband, daughter and girlfriends to seek help. When she did seek treatment, it was always on the sly. She kept her suffering hidden from her numerous fans. She felt there was only one answer:

It's impossible to survive a 155-foot fall from a bridge over an asphalt highway. In 2013, I reached the conclusion that the only direction left for my worthless life was down. I was convinced that a sudden fall from a high bridge was better than the slow-motion emotional decline I was enduring day by day.[197]

Fortunately, Judd remained in her car that day. Now, almost a decade later, she works to help others battling depression, urging them to understand that it's a handicap, not a failing, and that with help, they can endure.

I want to remind people, it's a disease of the brain, just like heart disease is a disease of the heart, and diabetes is a disease of the pancreas.... We have to find ways to cure it. There are researchers around the world working to find out about depression and about bipolar, and I just pray that any day I'm going to wake up and the headlines are going to say "Depression cured."
Until then, we have to have coping mechanisms, we have to have each other and we have to know some of the tools to use.[198]

Naomi Judd, beloved country music legend and actress with millions of fans, still lives from day to day, a constant reminder that depression—with help—can be endured.

Briana Browne

Peggy Browne was in a state of panic. Her daughter, Briana, was returning neither her calls nor texts. Something was wrong.

Briana had just returned from her first year of college in Kentucky to her Franklin, Tennessee home. Peggy was glad to have her back. She was also relieved, for Briana had been diagnosed with depression. Peggy was so concerned for her daughter's well-being that she made frequent trips to visit her on campus. Now, at least, Briana would be with her for the summer.

At 9:30 a.m. on May 13, 2016, just days after returning home, Briana told her mother she was going out for coffee. She never returned.

Terrified, Peggy went looking for her daughter. She drove to the Natchez Trace Parkway Bridge.[199] She found what she feared: Briana's car parked near the 145-foot guardrail. Briana wasn't in it. "I am the one who found her car on the bridge. I was looking over the side looking for her." Peggy's worst fears were confirmed: Briana had indeed leaped off the bridge.

But then a miracle occurred: Briana was still alive. She was found, rushed to the hospital and treated. Later, she would explain: "The trees are what broke my fall. I have read my own records. I broke most of my upper body, most things from the waist up. The [doctors] thankfully didn't have to do as much as they initially anticipated medically. It's a miracle, and it's amazing that I am alive. It's really crazy to wrap your mind around."

Others were not so fortunate. From 2006 to January 2021, there were thirty completed suicides at the Natchez Trace Parkway Bridge. Another twenty-seven were talked out of it by passersby or police officers.[200] Both Peggy and Briana understand this difficult fact. Peggy is in touch with others whose children and loved ones never returned from the bridge. She is overwhelmed with grief and gratitude. "I am left with these two strong emotions and a thankfulness that you can't describe. Every morning she walks in, I am like, 'She is still here.' My heart goes out so much for people who have lost lives. I feel strongly for them, but at the same time, I am so thankful I still have Briana."

Today, both mother and daughter work to make sure others have a better chance at survival, both psychologically and practically. Briana is open about the torments and dangers of depression, and both mother and daughter have worked to have the guardrails above the 145-foot drop heightened so as to discourage future suicides. As Briana noted, "I try to explain to people this mental state that you're in when you feel this way. There's no reasoning. But with the railing so low, it's so easy for people to stand up there and take their life."

Many suicides are irrational, impulsive decisions. If the person experiencing suicidal thoughts does not have easy access to a preferred death, it's possible the crisis will pass and the individual will get access to treatment.

The Natchez Trace Parkway Bridge. *Larry Yeiser.*

In other words, an impediment on the bridge—such as a raised barrier or netting—might buy enough time for the person to rethink their decision. Consequently, a number of activists have formed the Natchez Trace Barrier Coalition and have posted signs with the phone number for the National Suicide Prevention Lifeline, as well as emergency call boxes on either end of the bridge. The coalition continues to push for raised barriers, and with a groundswell of support, it hopes to have them in place by 2023.[201]

Chapter 13

EERIE MENAGERIE

ALL THROUGH THE YEARS, MONSTERS STALKED THE TRACE

For five hundred years, the people of the Trace have left remarkable stories in the historical record. But some of those stories lie just outside—or sometimes, miles outside—the bounds of veracity.

In nineteenth-century Tennessee and Mississippi, many of these stories appeared in respected newspapers—the same ones from which we know many crucial details of life along the early Trace. Readers learned that the Trace was the domain of an eerie menagerie—sea serpents swam in its rivers, spectral processions formed late at night, swarms of wolves hid in its forests and witches whispered in the ears of young women. The stories contained copious details, quotes from witnesses and seemingly scientific explanations. Readers loved them. But the discerning among them learned to read clues in the stories that revealed their apocryphal natures. The stories were often told in the present about occurrences from a near, but undefined, past. The stories were usually related secondhand to reporters. The sources themselves were always the most honest and respected people in their (usually distant) communities.

Most often, these stories formed around a certain ancient enemy of man, something that had caused real misery among settlers of the wilderness: snakes. So many fantastic snake stories appeared in newspapers that the phrase "snake story" came to be used as shorthand for a story that stretched—or broke—the truth.

Many snake stories have been told about the Natchez Trace and even encouraged by officials. The National Park Service erected, for example, a marker around mile 233 of the parkway for a place called "Witch Dance." The marker reads, "The old folks say the witches gathered here to dance and wherever their feet touched the ground the grass withered and died never to grow again." At Natchez (and every other old town on the Trace), ghosts haunt historic buildings. The ancient King's Tavern on Jefferson Street is haunted by the mistress of the old owner, a woman named Madeline who was murdered, appropriately, with a jeweled Spanish dagger.

Those more infamous tales often lack any foundation in the historical record. But the following five stories were all reported in respectable newspapers. Many of their readers believed the stories and were genuinely frightened. Now revived, the stories can provide fresh kindling for campfires along the Trace.

THE RAVENOUS PACK

Old Turner dragged his family down the Natchez Trace about the time the Choctaw moved out. He picked a spot off the road near the present site of Mathiston and built a crude cabin for himself, his wife and his two daughters.

In some ways, Turner and his family lived a life of deprivation, disconnected from society and left to provide for themselves. But in other ways, they lived a life of wealth. Because they were the vanguard of frontier settlers, game had not yet been exhausted. Other white Americans had to farm to feed themselves; Turner kept his larder full of venison. He spent his days hunting rather than hoeing.

He ranged one fall day into distant territory. He had walked five miles into swampland crossed by the Big Black River but had not spotted a deer. As the sun sank, one finally appeared. He marked it with his "flint and steel" and brought the animal down as he had so many others. It didn't take long for him to skin the deer and separate its hindquarters. He would use the hide as a vessel to carry the meat. With the sun now down, he started back through the swamp.

After walking for about a mile, Turner heard a sound behind him: the howling of a wolf. Not an unusual sound. Wolves—red wolves specifically—still roamed the forests of the Southeast then. But when he heard another howl and then another, he grew concerned. It seemed that they had found the site of his kill.

Turner increased his pace to a run. The wolves continued to howl, and their number seemed to be increasing. It seemed they were following him—

following the smell of the fresh meat. When he finally reached the clearing around his cabin after running some four miles, the wolves were only fifty yards behind him. Somehow, he managed to reach his cabin door without being caught; he slipped inside and collapsed on the floor. The wolves, whose number had grown large enough to constitute a "swarm," surrounded the cabin and began throwing their bodies into its sides.

The cabin—which must have been crude even by frontier standards—had a low roof that the wolves began to climb onto. The terrified family inside huddled underneath as the claws of the wolves rattled the roof's wooden shingles. The pack seemed bloodthirsty and determined. One tried climbing down the stick-and-mud chimney of the building. But when its head emerged in the family's fireplace, Turner's wife brought her axe down on it.

The family pushed all their furniture into the fireplace, blocking the only way in. For the rest of the night, they huddled awake as the wolves paced outside. When the sun rose and light filtered in through the rickety boards of the cabin, the wolves seemed to vanish all of a sudden. The sun's rise had dispersed the animals back into the woods.

Turner and his family must have meditated over their roasting venison that night. As they watched their meat sizzling, they must have thought, *We are just meat.* Turner must never again have felt as comfortable in the woods.[202]

THE RIVER MONSTER

Ed Baker's terrified men rowed his produce boat toward the landing at Natchez. It was the morning of December 10, 1877, and the night before had been long and full of terror.

The men moored the boat at the foot of Main Street and disembarked, happy to be on land again and thankful to be alive. The pilot, McCane George, helped his wife off the boat, and the two headed for Under-the-Hill, Natchez's seedy riverfront district. They were done crewing for Ed Baker. Dud Kelley and John Coughlin left as well. They had come closest to being destroyed the night before. When their nerves calmed, they would sit with a *Natchez Democrat* reporter and relate the details of the encounter.

All but one of the crewmen on Ed Baker's boat left that morning, vowing never to set foot on his boat again. By the time word of what had happened spread around Natchez, no other river boatmen would agree to crew his boat either. No one wanted to risk being devoured by the Mississippi River Monster.

"Cadmus and the Dragon," by Gustaf Tenggren, 1923. *Internet Archive.*

For four months, Natchez citizens had been living with the fear of an impending disaster. A slow-moving leviathan had been traveling downstream from St. Louis since August, eating cattle, attacking boats and terrifying river travelers. Natchez's citizens had clung to a gambler's hope that the monster would stop at Memphis or continue swimming to New Orleans without raising its ugly, imposing head near Natchez. But now those hopes had been dashed, for the monster had arrived.

Captain Baker found himself in the unenviable position of being Natchez's first victim. The attack had come the night before, as Baker's barge floated past an island in the river. The beast had been eighty feet away when it lifted its head eight feet above the water and set its eyes on Baker's boat. But it quickly closed the distance, churning the brown water into froth as it approached. Baker's terrified crew rushed inside the cabin of the boat, but two men had been sitting on the roof of the cabin and could not take cover. They were stuck there, watching as the monster approached. And it is from them that the citizens of Natchez would learn the horrible particulars of the monster that had claimed their section of the Mississippi.

Its back was covered with dark scales, like an alligator's. It had a slimy blue belly, like a catfish's, which it revealed when it sometimes turned like a corkscrew. It had a stringy black mane that trailed behind it as it swam. It had at least four long, paddle-tipped legs, maybe as many as six. Strangest of all, the beast had the head of a dog, with the emotive eyes and droopy ears of a basset hound. But it did not have a dog's mouth. Instead, it had a ten-foot-long beak that seemed to be made of ivory. The monster was some seventy-five feet long, all said.

Just as the monster reached the boat, it whipped its body to the right, striking the stern and sending an oar splashing into the water. The two crewmen on the roof could only watch in horror. Inexplicably, the monster swam away after striking the boat.

The attack petrified Baker's crew, and they were scarcely able to guide the ship to the Natchez landing. When the boat did arrive there, all the men aboard but one abandoned it. Captain Baker was stuck in Natchez, and no man would agree to step foot on his boat for fear of another attack.

The story of the river monster spread to newspapers across the country, eventually making the *New York Times*. But it seems that all the attention made the monster shy; when other newspaper editors began questioning the veracity of the Natchez story, the monster mysteriously vanished.[203]

O'Loony's Dream

Dennis O'Loony wandered into Port Gibson sometime in the late 1700s or early 1800s, a well-traveled and quick-witted drunk. He was Irish, and the people of Port Gibson took great pleasure in mocking his speech and habits. The quantity of "krater" he consumed, and the frequency with which he consumed it, further harmed his reputation.

Some time after he arrived in Port Gibson, the people of the town were swept up in a religious fervor. It seemed that many souls were saved. This might have coincided with the visit of Lorenzo Dow, the famous long-haired evangelist who held Mississippi's first campground revival near the town in 1804. In any case, O'Loony dedicated himself to Christianity as well. But he did not stop drinking.

One night, after consuming so much alcohol that he had achieved the "most beastly state of drunkenness," O'Loony stumbled on a pile of bricks in the road, fell flat on his face and was rendered unconscious. Some young Port Gibson residents took the opportunity to paint his face with turpentine and lamp-black (in the morning, he would wake up and people would ask him why he looked so blue).

But while O'Loony's body lay there, his consciousness traveled to another realm. O'Loony realized that he had died and that it was time for him to find the gates of heaven and ask St. Peter for admittance. He walked a celestial plain for four days, feeling sad that he had nothing to drink. He finally arrived at a tall wall encrusted with jewels "as thick as feathers on the back of a goose." He made a fist and beat it against the gates before him.

St. Peter's head rose over the wall. He asked O'Loony in a calm, sweet voice where he had come from and what he wanted. He was from Port Gibson, O'Loony said, and he wanted to enter the gates and sit beside St. Peter. He wanted to pray for the souls of the lost. St. Peter nodded and told O'Loony to wait a moment while he checked his record books.

O'Loony waited for an hour. When St. Peter lifted his head again, his sweet and peaceful countenance had grown twisted and enraged. St. Peter shouted at O'Loony in a voice louder than thunder, accusing him of trying to lie his way into heaven. O'Loony was a "thieving spalpeen," St. Peter shouted.

Taken aback, O'Looney told St. Peter that he would never do such a thing. May the devil take his soul if he had ever tried to deceive him, he said.

"Profile of a Vagabond," by James C. McGuire, 1864. *Metropolitan Museum of Art.*

"Why, didn't you tell me you was from Port Gibson?" St. Peter asked.

"Yes, yer reverence, I did," O'Loony said. "And I'll stick to it if I die by it. I came from that same beautiful place, and if I'm not mistaken you've got many of its citizens wid you now."

St. Peter grew even angrier, and his face turned as black as tar. His voice grew so terrible that it made O'Loony tremble. "You're a lying spalpeen, for I've just been looking over my books, and I find that there is no person here from Port Gibson at all," St. Peter rumbled. "Nor do I believe that any such place exists!"

St. Peter's revelation awoke O'Looney from his krater-induced coma, and he climbed up from the street. He resolved that day to leave. He could not stay in a town that had never sent a single delegate to the "place where peace and joy and good will to all men reign forever" and whose presence was not even recorded on its maps.[204]

Uktena

In the 1800s, Tennesseans were titillated by actual snake stories, which appeared frequently in newspapers across the state. Nashville readers seemed as interested as anyone, and innumerable snake stories were published there.

There was the one about the Irish woman who moved to Tennessee and, being unfamiliar with snakes because there were none in her home country, swallowed what she thought were two partridge eggs while out on a hike. The eggs hatched inside her stomach, and two rattlesnakes grew into healthy and active specimens, causing her much discomfort. There was the one about the "milk snake" who vexed a farmer by sucking all the milk from his contented cow's udder. There was the one about the time it rained snakes in Memphis. And the one about the woman who gave birth to two half-human, half-snake children. From the waist up, they were completely reptilian and played by crawling on the floor, hissing and striking at each other with their fangs.[205]

Most of the stories seemed to originate in the Appalachians, but in 1868, the residents of Nashville learned that a singularly wonderful snake had taken up residence on their doorstep in Williamson County to the south. The *Republican Banner* was the paper to break the news of the snake. Two men had been riding through a section of hills east of Franklin called the Burke Knobs. They rode upon what they thought was a pole lying across the road. But the pole began to move, lifting itself over a fence before slithering into a field.

It was a snake, thirty or forty feet long and about as big around as a man's thigh. The snake moved at a leisurely pace, stopping to sun itself and lifting its head fifteen feet in the air occasionally to survey the landscape. The men watched it for two hours. It caught and ate a rabbit at one point before lowing like a cow and slithering into a burrow in the side of a hill.

The two men reported what they had seen to their neighbors, and the neighbors constructed a fifty-foot-long timber box and lodged it in the snake's burrow. They would lure the snake out with a piece of mutton.

That was all there was to the story—there was a giant snake living south of Nashville. The story, reported in detail by the paper, was unusual, but it did not seem impossible. Exotic snakes were known to exist, and one Nashville resident even hypothesized that the "Big Snake" was a boa constrictor that had escaped from a traveling menagerie some thirty years before (the anaconda, the largest snake in the world, can grow up to thirty feet long and weigh 550 pounds).

The story proved to be popular, and the *Republican* continued the narrative in subsequent installments. The snake's tail became an alligator's tail, and the snake grew four tusks. Eventually, the beast was shot, skinned and stuffed with sawdust. The slayers of the animal planned to exhibit it in Nashville. Readers hoping to get a glimpse of the taxidermied specimen were inevitably disappointed.[206]

Long before any printing press reached Nashville, the Cherokee knew such snakes as *uktena*. They were monstrous horned snakes first created by men to kill the Sun. They lived in the high mountains. The *uktena* had glittering scales and a diamond crystal on its forehead. The snake had the power to mesmerize humans, who—if they saw the creature—would walk toward it to their deaths.

A Cherokee warrior named Agan-uni tsi killed an *uktena* and took its diamond crystal. The crystal possessed such power that it had to be fed once a week with the blood of small animals and twice a year with the blood of a deer or bear. If he didn't complete the ritual, the crystal would rise from the jar in which it was kept and assume the form of fire and murder a person—perhaps Agan-uni tsi himself.

But the crystal also granted him powers. Agan-uni tsi could be assured of success in hunting, farming and lovemaking as long as he possessed the crystal. And by peering into the crystal, he could see the future—whether a sick person would live or die, whether a child would grow to be old or whether a warrior would perish in battle. He might have stared into the crystal hundreds of years ago and seen a confusing vision: a pale-faced and bearded man, giggling over strange symbols on a sheaf.[207]

The Undeparted

John Rains almost did not make it to Nashville. He was taking his family, with all his cattle and horses, west to Kentucky. But at the Cumberland Gap he ran into an old acquaintance: James Robertson. Robertson told him that he should head south to the Cumberland River. It was pristine country, and Robertson was about to establish a settlement there. Trusting in providence, Rains followed his friend. He arrived at the frozen river on Christmas Day 1779.

In the following decades, Rains would farm the land he had claimed just outside Nashville and watch the town grow up from wilderness. He survived the precarious years of the Cumberland settlements, when Indian attacks came frequently. He grew to an old age.

In the 1810s, Nashville was still a tiny settlement, with fewer than three thousand residents. But it was large enough to provide old John Rains with a night out. Sometime around 1815 or 1816, Rains departed a gathering in Nashville and made for his home about a mile from town. It was dark and late, so when he passed an old log house that had once been used as a blacksmith's shop, the bright light shining from its windows was a curious beacon. Rains dismounted and walked to the front door. He peeked through a window and was surprised to see that the blacksmith's shop was once again in operation.

But the scene he beheld looking through the window was all wrong. The two people he saw hammering nails in the middle of the shop were old friends of his...but they had died not long before. The clothes they wore were the same ones they had been wearing when they died. And though they hammered at an anvil in the middle of the shop, there was no anvil there—it had been taken from the shop long ago. Two others whom Rains did not recognize also stood in the shop, observing the spectral hammering.

Rains, who had survived decades on the hostile frontier, was not frightened by the scene. He stood there watching for a while and then mounted his horse and headed back for his house. But his horse only traveled a little ways before stopping. No matter how hard and how many times he struck the mare, she would not take another step forward. He resolved to turn around and sleep in Nashville that night.

When Rains told others what he had seen, they figured he had been shown the scene by God as proof of an afterlife. The vision was meant to deepen Rains's faith. But such a vision could be interpreted in many ways. Perhaps the vision had been a warning to Rains: *Travel the road tonight, and you will join these ghostly smiths.* Perhaps the mare knew this.

Or perhaps the souls toiling in the blacksmith's shop had been judged unworthy to enter paradise. Perhaps, like Dennis O'Loony, they had been rejected by God and were stuck wandering the Natchez Trace, seeding stories that would grow for ages.[208]

NOTES

Chapter 1

1. De la Vega, *La Florida*, 446–64.
2. Barnett, *Natchez Indians*, 4–7.
3. Hudson, *Knights of Spain, Warriors of the Sun*, 390–94.
4. Duncan, *Hernando de Soto*, 38–39.
5. Payne-Gallwey, *Crossbow*, 5–10; De la Vega, *La Florida*, 334–37.
6. White, "Artifacts and Archaeology," 44–53.
7. De la Vega, *La Florida*, 337–48.
8. Shaffer, *Native Americans Before 1492*, 70–71.
9. Barnett, *Natchez Indians*, 4–7; De la Vega, *La Florida*, 337–48.
10. National Park Service, National Register of Historic Places Registration Form: Emerald Mound.

Chapter 2

11. Penicaut, *Fleur de Lys and Calumet*, 92–95.
12. Ibid., 83.
13. Ibid., 86.
14. Ibid., 80–87.
15. Myers, *1729*, 131; Dumont, *Memoir of Lieutenant Dumont*, 358–61.
16. Barnett, *Natchez Indians*.
17. Penicaut, *Fleur de Lys and Calumet*, 92, footnote 11.
18. Myers, *1729*, 126.
19. Barnett, *Natchez Indians*, 3–21. James F. Barnett Jr., Natchez Indian expert, details a naval battle in the Mississippi River between Spanish conquistadors and the predecessors of the Natchez in 1543.

20. Penicaut, *Fleur de Lys and Calumet*, 92–94.
21. Barnett, *Natchez Indians*, 45–46.
22. Cushman, *History of the Choctaw*, 438.
23. Barnett, *Natchez Indians*, 41–42. The other villages were Flower, Tiou, Griga, Jenzenqaque, White Apple and Flour.
24. Myers, *1729*, 127, 129.
25. Ibid., 131–32; Dumont, *Memoir of Lieutenant Dumont*, 358–61; Penicaut, *Fleur de Lys and Calumet*, 94–96.

Chapter 3

26. Officially, there is no record of a person being killed by alligator in Mississippi. However, it would be naïve to suspect that there were no unrecorded deaths during the pioneer days or before. There is plenty of evidence that such deaths occurred in neighboring Louisiana.
27. Myers, *1729*, 82.
28. Ibid., 81.
29. Becherer, "Photos: See Massive 12-Foot Long, 672-Pound Alligator."
30. Williams, "Record Alligator Caught Near Natchez."
31. Myers, *1729*, 81.
32. Also known as the water moccasin.
33. *Natchez Weekly Courier*, "The King Snake," May 10, 1848.
34. Ibid. As improbable as this story sounds, it was published in a respectable paper as truth. Furthermore, the rattlesnake likely would have coiled up and begun shaking its rattle upon seeing a kingsnake in the area.
35. Dr. Elizabeth James, the emergency department director at Natchez Regional Medical Center, suggests not attempting to kill the snake that caused the initial snakebite: "A lot of times people get bitten again trying to do that. If you can take a picture of the snake from a safe distance, that is fine." She added that doctors can tell if a snake is venomous by the reaction of the bitten. Shelton, "Three Bites in Three Months."
36. Shelton, "Three Bites in Three Months."
37. Because of modern medicine, the odds of dying of a venomous snake bite in the United States is minimal. Of the seven to eight thousand venomous bites per year, only five to six are fatal. University of Florida, Department of Wildlife Ecology and Conservation.
38. *Weekly Democrat*, "Antidote for Snake Poison," September 17, 1866.
39. Shelton, "Three Bites in Three Months."
40. Clark, *Voices from an Early American Convent*, 63.
41. "Letter to Union Chambers of Commerce, Washington Post," 53.
42. Moore, "Claiborne County, Mississippi and the Yellow Fever Epidemics"; National Park Service, "Rocky Springs Town Site, Milepost 54.8."
43. Atlas Obscura, "Grave of Florence Irene Ford"; "Strange Graves at Natchez City Cemetery," YouTube.

Chapter 4

44. Ramsey, *Annals of Tennessee to the End of the Eighteenth Century*, 445–52.
45. *Short Description of the Tennassee Government*.
46. *South-western Monthly*, "Narrative of William Hall," 331–36; Brown, *Old Frontiers*, 259–63.
47. *Short Description of the Tennassee Government*.
48. Nichols, "Alexander Cameron, British Agent"; Kitchin and Cadell, *Map of the European Settlements in North America*.
49. Davidson, *The Tennessee*, 182–200.
50. Brown, *Old Frontiers*, 259–63.
51. St. Jean, "How the Chickasaws Saved the Cumberland Settlement."
52. Kappler, "Treaty with the Chickasaw."
53. Brown, *Old Frontiers*, 259–63; Ramsey, *Annals of Tennessee to the End of the Eighteenth Century*, 462–72.
54. *South-western Monthly*, "Narrative of William Hall," 331–36.
55. St. Jean, "How the Chickasaws Saved the Cumberland Settlement."

Chapter 5

56. Davis, *Three Roads to the Alamo*, 162–63.
57. *Natchez Weekly Democrat*, "Duel—Assassination," September 21, 1827.
58. The "Sandbar Fight" has fascinated historians and history buffs for generations. Its factual details, however, are difficult to untangle.
59. Meachem, *American Lion*, 298–99.
60. Ibid., 512. After an investigation, Poindexter was exonerated, and Richard Lawrence was declared mentally insane. The latter lived out the rest of his life in a mental asylum. One hundred years later, researchers conducted a field test on each pistol, both of which fired properly on the first try. They calculated the odds of both pistols failing to detonate the powder was 1 in 125,000. At less than ten feet distance, Andrew Jackson should have been the United States' first assassinated president. History, "Andrew Jackson Narrowly Escapes Assassination."
61. Cisco, "Historic Sumner County, TN."
62. Every president makes use of the spoils system, and yet Andrew Jackson is erroneously cursed with instituting the custom in the United States.
63. Cisco, "Historic Sumner County, TN." Gwin's wife, Nancy, was dying of tuberculosis. Gwin was told that her only hope was to move to a dryer climate, hence the move to Mississippi. Nancy died in Clinton 1833.
64. Poindexter was born in Virginia.
65. Caldwell had fought a duel in 1829 with John B. Peyton when the latter voted against moving the state capital to Caldwell's hometown, Clinton. Caldwell's previous two duels were fought on the same field.

66. Although at the First Constitutional Convention of 1817 a proposal was made to make dueling a disqualification for public office, the proposal was rejected thirty-seven to six. Thomspon, "Old-Style Battles Once Fought On State Soil."
67. Some sources say that each duelist received six pistols. Regardless, the outcome was the same.
68. Jerry Mitchell, "History of High Court Justices in Miss. Reveals Tradition of Impropriety," *Clarion-Ledger*, May 5, 2003.
69. Issaquena County, Mississippi, History and Genealogy.
70. The meal is pure conjecture. But...they were in New Orleans; is it really conjecture?
71. Lane, *Architecture of the Old South*, 178–79.
72. *Easter Clarion*, May 25, 1859.
73. Today in Mississippi, "Mississippi Seen."
74. *Mississippi Baptist*, May 26, 1859, page 3, column 2.
75. Helen ended up marrying George Harris, a Confederate chaplain, in 1862. The couple had three children and moved about on account of his vocation. Helen ended up dying near Rolling Fork, Mississippi, at the home George built her—Mount Helena, atop an Indian burial mound—in 1917. She is buried at Mound Cemetery in Rolling Fork.

Chapter 6

76. Dow, *History of Cosmopolite*, 213–21.
77. Foreman and Starrett, *Hidden History of Natchez*; *Regulations and Instructions Relating to His Majesty's Service at Sea*, 61–68.
78. Davis, *Way through the Wilderness*, 14–16.
79. *Gazette*, "Removal," September 28, 1802.
80. *Green's Impartial Observer*, "Just Received...," January 24, 1801.
81. *Herald*, "Prices Current," September 27, 1802.
82. Hudson, *Southeastern Indians*, 272–75; Trotta, "Food, Function and Fashion," 2–5.
83. Hudson, *Southeastern Indians*, 272–75.
84. Holt, "Hunting and Fishing."
85. Hudson, *Southeastern Indians*, 275–79.
86. Holt, "Hunting and Fishing."
87. Hudson, *Southeastern Indians*, 292–95.
88. *Evening Post*, "While Passing through the Choctaw, Chickasaw, and Cherokee Nations of Indians," September 1, 1803.
89. Phelps, "Stands and Travel Accommodations."
90. Foreman and Starrett, *Hidden History of Natchez*; Bertram, "Great Age."
91. Phelps, "Stands and Travel Accommodations."
92. Tony L. Turnbow, e-mail message to authors, September 3, 2021.
93. *Mississippi Messenger*, "House of Entertainment," November 11, 1806; *Mississippi Messenger*, "Notice to Travellers," June 15, 1808.
94. Brown, *Indian Invention of New World Foods*, 8–9.

95. Ibid.
96. *Mississippi Free Trader*, "Natchez Prices Current," November 7, 1822.
97. *Mississippi Free Trader*, "Steele's Spring," June 29, 1819.

Chapter 7

98. Herodotus, quoted in Michener, *Drifters*, 9.
99. The following account of the Battles of Ogoula Tchetoka and Ackia come from three sources: Cobb, Smith, Lieb and Legg, "Ackia and Ogoula Tchetoka"; King, *Jean Baptiste Le Moyne Sieur De Bienville*; and Cushman, *History of the Choctaw*.
100. Ericson, "Famous Mobilian You Should Know."
101. Present-day Amory, Mississippi.
102. Present-day south Tupelo.
103. Present-day Memphis.
104. Ogoula Tchetoka, in present-day northwest Tupelo.
105. Maybe Father Senat led his companions willingly into the flames, maybe not. Regardless, he does appear to have died encouraging his companions and in the manner expected of any brave Chickasaw or Choctaw. Indiana Catholic History, "Father Senat Murdered."
106. Brad Lieb, tribal archaeologist for Chickasaw Nation's Department of Culture and Humanities, Division of Heritage Preservation, argues that the village of Ackia was not prepared for Bienville's attack. Unlike most of the Chickasaw Nation, Ackia—being on the periphery—had a solid trade relationship with the French. They were, in fact, almost taken by surprise. Lieb pointed out that rather than one hundred warriors present at the battle, there were likely only forty—the rest were out hunting. Lieb, "Battle of Ackia."
107. Robert Leckie, quoted in Buckley and Nokes, *Explorers of the American West*, 40.
108. Soodalter, "Untouchable Agent 13."
109. More than a century later, historians uncovered documents that had been sent to Madrid from Havana that finally revealed that Wilkinson had been a double agent and in the pay of Spain all along.
110. Turnbow, *Hardened to Hickory*, 97.
111. National Public Radio, "Man Who Double-Crossed the Founders." The Spanish trekking party got to within sixty miles of Lewis and Clark. Turnbow, 100.
112. Just in case Jackson did run into Wilkinson, he had brought along a pair of dueling pistols. Knowing how Wilkinson appreciated luxury, he made sure that his guns were packed with the finest powder so as to impress the rake before he killed him. Turnbow, *Hardened to Hickory*, 340.
113. Maass, "Army's Disaster at Terre aux Boeufs."
114. Turnbow, *Hardened to Hickory*, 368. Four days earlier, Private John Drum was also buried with full military honors.
115. Ibid., 375.
116. Ibid., 397.
117. Ibid., 429.

118. Ibid.
119. Moore, "Death of General Lloyd Tilghman."
120. Ibid.
121. Find a Grave, "Robert Theodore Cooper."
122. Daniel, "Lewis County."

Chapter 8

123. Corbitt, "James Colbert and the Spanish Claims," 457–59.
124. Braden, "Colberts and the Chickasaw Nation," 222–49; Colbert, "James Logan Colbert of the Chickasaws," 82–96.
125. Corbitt, "James Colbert and the Spanish Claims," 457–59.
126. Ibid.
127. Rothert, *Outlaws of Cave-in-Rock*, 157–258; Bell, *Samuel Mason*, 1–26.
128. Fennell, "Man Behind WorldCom."
129. Lohr, "Long Distance Visionary"; Schiesel, "MCI Accepts Offer of $36.5 Billion."
130. Hau, "Big Company Leaves Small Town in the Lurch."
131. Schiesel, "Re-Engineering of Bernie Ebbers"; Chambers, "Yacht Waits Out Storms in Charleston."
132. Eichenwald, "For WorldCom, Acquisitions Were Behind Its Rise and Fall"; Abelson, "Gorging on a Diet of Deals."
133. Eichenwald, "For WorldCom, Acquisitions Were Behind Its Rise and Fall."
134. Bayot, "Ebbers Sentenced to 25 Years in Prison for $11 Billion Fraud."
135. Kadlec, "WorldCon."

Chapter 9

136. Really, the central United States, but it was the "West" in 1811.
137. Feldman, *When the Mississippi Ran Backwards*, 149–50.
138. Ibid., 9.
139. Ibid., 178.
140. Ibid.
141. Turnbow, *Hardened to Hickory*, 158.
142. Feldman, *When the Mississippi Ran Backwards*, 160 and 172.
143. Ibid., 175–76. The above descriptions apply to regions affected at levels VI–VII, both of which large sections of the Trace would have experienced due to its proximity to the epicenters.
144. The warrior branch of Creek, as opposed to the white (peace) faction.
145. William Henry Harrison and John Tyler ("Tippecanoe and Tyler, too!").
146. Davis, *Way through the Wilderness*, 56.
147. Elvispresleymusic.com.
148. The highest possible rating on the Fujita scale

149. Reed, "Witness Describes Tupelo Tornado."
150. *Coffeeville Courier*, "Tupelo Worst Hit: 200 Killed: Many Injured: Thousands Left Homeless," April 10, 1936.
151. *Coffeeville Courier*, "Storm Picks Chickens: Blows Curbing from Well," April 10, 1936.
152. Parsons, "Houses with History." Many estimate that the death toll was significantly higher, perhaps as high as 350. The most conservative estimate is 216.
153. *Greenwood Commonwealth*, "Storm Victims Are Piled in Undertaking Parlors," April 6, 1936.
154. Tupelo was the first city to receive cheap electricity from the Tennessee Valley Authority.
155. *Greenwood Commonwealth*, "Storm Victims Are Piled."
156. *Enterprise-Journal*, "500 Attend Jim Burrough Family Rites," April 10, 1936; Coppenbarger, "13 Coffins in 1 Grave."
157. Lyrics.com, https://www.lyrics.com/lyric/8067551/Acappella/In+the+Sweet+By+and+By.
158. Parsons, "Houses with History."
159. With a brief stop in Pascagoula, Mississippi, and Parchman Prison.
160. Elvispresleymusic.com.

Chapter 10

161. *Vicksburg Whig*, "An American Pigeon Roost," September 23, 1831.
162. Pollock, "Passenger Pigeon," 97–98.
163. Folsom, "Biological Sketch with Excerpts from His Diary," 430–31; Cushman, *History of the Choctaw*, 388–89.
164. Phelps, "Stands and Travel Accommodations," 1–54.
165. Edward J. Burnham, ed., "Fate of the Passenger Pigeon," *Nature Study* 4 (1904).
166. *Vicksburg American*, "Tragedy of Animal Life," May 26, 1903; Pollock, "Passenger Pigeon," 97–98.
167. Wright, "Some Early Records of the Passenger Pigeon," 428–33.
168. Neumann, "Human-Wildlife Competition and the Passenger Pigeon," 389–410.
169. Steadman, "And Live on Pigeon Pie"; Pollock, "Passenger Pigeon," 97–98; *Vicksburg Evening Post*, "An Immense Pigeon Roost," November 9, 1886.
170. *Vicksburg Whig*, "Important Disclosures," December 17, 1835.
171. *Star-Herald*, "Lone Pigeon Left," January 20, 1911.
172. *Clarion-Ledger*, "Passenger Pigeons," June 15, 1947; Malone, *Chickasaw Nation*, 89–95.
173. Hung et al., "Drastic Population Fluctuations," 10,636–641; Wright, "Some Early Records of the Passenger Pigeon," 428–33.

Chapter 11

174. U.S. Department of the Interior, National Park Service, *Natchez Trace Travel*, https://www.natcheztracetravel.com/natchez-trace-mississippi/vicksburg-port-gibson-ms/241-grindstone-ford.html.
175. *Mississippi Free Trader*, "Dreadful Accident," July 17, 1821.
176. Burnett did leave behind one surviving grandson—Daniel Burnet Patterson—who was also buried in the family plot when he died in 1848.
177. The vignette about the Natchez Drug Company fire of 1908 was pieced together from the following *Natchez Democrat* articles: "Five Funerals Held Yesterday," March 17, 1908; "Card of Thanks," March 17, 1908; "Work Nearing End; Eight Bodies Found," March 18, 1908; "Explosion Was Caused by Gas," March 19, 1908; and "The Last Chapter," March 19, 1908. See also Woodrick, "Lost in Flames."
178. Some accounts have Hoskins jumping from the window to avoid the flames. However, the jury inquest of March 17 declared that he had fallen accidentally.
179. Chambliss must have thought that Mrs. Ketteringham, the sixth female victim, would be provided for by her husband.
180. The writers can find no record of Willie Kates, and we cannot locate his grave. We hope that a more talented historian can dig into his story—it would be a wonderful contribution to the field of history, as well as justice for Mr. Kates if his grave could be honored as well. At the time, the *Natchez Democrat* reported, "It is probable that all of the bodies, with the exception of that of Cleve Laub and the negro boy, and Uriah Hoskins, will find sepulture in this spot. The Company has announced its intention of erecting a handsome and appropriate monument above the resting place of the victims."
181. One of the gunmen firing over Sam's casket was his brother Joseph. Joseph also worked tirelessly with the Hook and Ladder Brigade and doubtless saved several lives that afternoon as his brother's body burned inside the building.

Chapter 12

182. Guice, *By His Own Hand?*, 64.
183. The entirety of the following vignette on Meriwether Lewis comes from one source: Guice's *By His Own Hand?* Using one source is usually not good historical work—unless the one source is compiled in the way Guice's work is. Guice brings together several prominent historians and places Lewis's death on trial. Each writer is given his own space, and so, the work is biased on the micro level and unbiased on the macro. In short, Guice produced the definitive (inconclusive) work on the death of Meriwether Lewis. Ironically, the present writers side against Guice. We believe that Lewis was the victim of suicide, not murder or a conspiracy. However, the evidence in favor of murder cannot be discounted. We strongly urge any student of history to read Guice's work. It is an exemplar of historiography. (For the sake of the ever-present word count to which most authors are beholden, know that we did not footnote every paragraph. However,

150

the entirety of this vignette came from Guice's work, whose contributors are preeminent Meriwether Lewis historians, including Elliott West, Clay S. Jenkinson, James J. Holmberg, John D.W. Guice and Jay H. Buckley.)

184. Milepost 385.9.
185. Lewis, journal entry, August 18, 1805, quoted in Guice, *By His Own Hand?*, 88.
186. Guice, *By His Own Hand?*, 65.
187. There are several potential murderers of Lewis among the homicide advocates; James Wilkinson is one of them. After all, he had advised Spain to "end" the Corps of Discovery years before.
188. Guice, *By His Own Hand?*, 123. Murder theorists are quick to point out that James Neelly, the man who accompanied Lewis up the Trace, was sent by Wilkinson to be Lewis's escort. Neelly would also write to Jefferson on October 18, 1809: "I have got in my possession…some Vouchers for expenditures of Public money for a Bill which he said had been protested by Secy. Of War, and of which act to his death, he repeatedly complained." Guice, *By His Own Hand?*, 150–51.
189. Modern-day Memphis.
190. Guice, *By His Own Hand?*, 40–41.
191. It is likely that he was suffering from malaria.
192. Guice, *By His Own Hand?*, 44.
193. We do not know what these horses carried. Perhaps the journals of the expedition?
194. Alexander Wilson letter to Alexander Lawson of Natchez, May 28, 1811, quoted in Guice, *By His Own Hand?*, 157.
195. Guice, *By His Own Hand?*, 115.
196. Judd, *River of Time*, 85.
197. Ibid., 1.
198. Whitall, "Naomi Judd Wants to Banish the Stigma of Mental Illness."
199. Milepost 438.
200. Tiede, "Amid Recent Suicide Scares."
201. The story of Briana Brown's suicide attempt, recovery and mission can be found in the following articles: West, "She Is the Only Suicide Survivor"; West, "They Lost Loved Ones to Suicide"; and Frist, "Tennessee Is Home to One of the Deadliest Parks."

Chapter 13

202. *Atlanta Constitution*, "Chased by Wolves," October 23, 1886.
203. *New York Times*, "The Mississippi River Monster," December 27, 1877; *St. Louis Globe-Democrat*, "The River Reptile," September 21, 1877.
204. *Port Gibson Herald*, "Dennis O'Loony and His Dhrame," September 1, 1842.
205. *Nashville Union and American*, "Snakes!" July 10, 1874; *Tennessean*, "Cow Gives No Milk; Snake Getting It All," July 9, 1929; *Tennessean*, "The Toughest Snake Story We Ever Heard," November 17, 1866; *Tennessean*, "Shower of Snakes at Memphis," January 17, 1877.

206. *Nashville Banner*, "The Triune Monster—Most Famous Snake Story Ever Published in State of Tennessee," May 17, 1931.

207. Conley, *Cherokee Medicine Man*, 20–23.

208. *Clarion and Tennessee State Gazette*, "Of Animal Mechanism," July 6, 1819.

BIBLIOGRAPHY

Articles

Abelson, Reed. "Gorging on a Diet of Deals." *New York Times,* July 5, 1998.

Barnett, Jim. "The Natchez Indians." *Mississippi History Now.* http://www.mshistorynow.mdah.ms.gov/articles/4/the-natchez-indians.

Bayot, Jennifer. "Ebbers Sentenced to 25 Years in Prison for $11 Billion Fraud." *New York Times,* July 13, 2005.

Bertram, Jack. "The Great Age: The Rise and Fall of the Natchez Trace." *Clarion-Ledger,* May 25, 2000.

Braden, Guy B. "The Colberts and the Chickasaw Nation." *Tennessee Historical Quarterly* 17, no. 3 (1958).

Chambers, Susan. "Yacht Waits Out Storms in Charleston." *The World,* January 14, 1995.

Cobb, Charles R., Steven D. Smith, Brad Lieb and James B. Legg. "Ackia and Ogoula Tchetoka: Defining Two Battlefields of the 1736 French and Chickasaw War in Southeastern North America." *Journal of Field Archaeology* (August 2017). https://www.researchgate.net/publication/319295574_Ackia_and_Ogoula_Tchetoka_Defining_Two_Battlefields_of_the_1736_French_and_Chickasaw_War_in_Southeastern_North_America.

Colbert, Richard A. "James Logan Colbert of the Chickasaws: The Man and the Myth." *North Carolina Genealogical Society Journal* 20, no. 2 (1994).

Coppenbarger, H.L. "13 Coffins in 1 Grave as Tupelo Dead Are Buried." *Clarion-Ledger,* April 8, 1936.

Corbitt, D.C. "James Colbert and the Spanish Claims to the East Bank of the Mississippi." *Mississippi Valley Historical Review* 24, no. 4 (1938).

Eichenwald, Kurt. "For WorldCom, Acquisitions Were Behind Its Rise and Fall." *New York Times,* August 8, 2002.

Ericson, Sally Pearsall. "A Famous Mobilian You Should Know: Bienville, Our Tattooed Founding Father." Alabama.com. https://www.al.com/live/2013/10/a_famous_mobilian_you_should_k.html.

Fennell, Tom. "The Man Behind WorldCom." *Maclean's* 110, no. 42 (1997).

Folsom, Willis S. "A Biological Sketch with Excerpts from His Diary." From *Chronicles of Oklahoma*. Vol. 3. Oklahoma City: Oklahoma Historical Society, 1925.

Hau, Louis. "Big Company Leaves Small Town in the Lurch." *Tampa Bay Times*, June 1, 2002.

Holt, Julie. "Hunting and Fishing: A (Native) American Tradition." *Illinois Antiquity* 45, no, 3 (2010).

Hung, Chih-Ming, et al. "Drastic Population Fluctuations Explain the Rapid Extinction of the Passenger Pigeon." *Proceedings of the National Academy of Sciences of the United States of America* 111, no. 29 (2014).

Kadlec, Daniel. "WorldCon." *TIME*, May 6, 2002.

Lohr, Steve. "A Long Distance Visionary." *New York Times*, October 2, 1997.

Maass, John R. "The Army's Disaster at Terre Aux Boeufs, 1809." *Army History* (Fall 2012). https://www.jstor.org/stable/26298831?seq=2#metadata_info_tab_contents.

Neumann, Thomas W. "Human-Wildlife Competition and the Passenger Pigeon." *Human Ecology* 13, no. 4 (1985).

Nichols, John L. "Alexander Cameron, British Agent Among the Cherokee, 1764–1781." *South Carolina Historical Magazine* 97, no. 2 (1996).

Parsons, Ginna. "Houses with History: 1936 Tornado Destroyed, Damaged Many Older Homes." *Daily Journal*, April 5, 2011.

Phelps, Dawson A. "Stands and Travel Accommodations of the Natchez Trace." *Journal of Mississippi History* 10, no. 1 (1948).

Pollock, Christal. "The Passenger Pigeon." *Journal of Avian Medicine and Surgery* 17, no. 2 (2003).

Reed, William. "Witness Describes Tupelo Tornado." *Greenwood Commonwealth*, April 6, 1936.

Schiesel, Seth. "MCI Accepts Offer of $36.5 Billion; Deal Sets Record." *New York Times*, November 11, 1997.

———. "The Re-Engineering of Bernie Ebbers." *New York Times*, April 27, 1998.

Soodalter, Ron. "Untouchable Agent 13." HistoryNet, 2018. https://www.historynet.com/untouchable-agent-13.htm.

South-western Monthly 1. "Narrative of William Hall" (1852).

St. Jean, Wendy. "How the Chickasaws Saved the Cumberland Settlement in the 1790s." *Tennessee Historical Quarterly* 68, no. 1 (2009).

Steadman, David W. "And Live on Pigeon Pie." *New York State Conservationist* 50, no. 5 (1996).

Thompson, Sue. "Old-Style Battles once Fought On State Soil." *Clarion-Ledger*, August 13, 1971.

Trotta, Paul. "Food, Function and Fashion: Native Americans and Whitetail Deer." *New York State Conservationist* 61, no. 2 (2006): 2–5.

West, Emily R. "They Lost Loved Ones to Suicide on the Natchez Trace Bridge. They Say Better Barriers Could Prevent More Tragedies." *The Tennessean,* January 25, 2019.

———. "She Is the Only Suicide Survivor of the Natchez Trace Bridge. She Doesn't Want Anyone Else to Jump." *The Tennessean,* May 29, 2019.

Whitall, Susan. "Naomi Judd Wants to Banish the Stigma of Mental Illness." *Detroit News,* June 11, 2018.

White, Fred A. "Artifacts and Archaeology from the Conquistador Hernando de Soto's Potano Encampment and the Lost Franciscan Mission." *International Journal of Archaeology* 4, no. 4 (2016).

Wright, Albert Hazen. "Some Early Records of the Passenger Pigeon." *The Auk* 27, no. 4 (1910).

Books

Barnett, James F., Jr. *The Natchez Indians: A History to 1735.* Jackson: University Press of Mississippi, 2007.

Bell, Raymond Martin. *Samuel Mason, 1739–1803.* Washington, PA: R.M. Bell, 1985.

Brown, Elsworth. *Indian Invention of New World Foods.* Knoxville: University of Tennessee Press, 1957.

Brown, John P. *Old Frontiers.* Kingsport, TN: Southern Publishers, 1938.

Buckley, Jay, and Jeffrey Nokes. *Explorers of the American West: Mapping the World through Primary Documents.* ABC-CLIO, Illustrated Edition, 2016.

Clark, Emily. *Voices from an Early American Convent: Marie Madeleine Hachard and the New Orleans Ursulines, 1727–1760.* Baton Rouge: Louisiana State University Press, 2009.

Coates, Robert M. *The Outlaw Years.* Gretna, LA: Pelican Publishing Company, 2002.

Conley, Robert J. *Cherokee Medicine Man.* Norman: University of Oklahoma Press, 2005.

Cushman, H.B. *History of the Choctaw, Chickasaw and Natchez Indians.* Norman: University of Oklahoma Press, 1999.

Daniels, Jonathan. *The Devil's Backbone: The Story of the Natchez Trace.* Gretna, LA: Pelican Publishing Company, 1998.

Davidson, Donald. *The Tennessee.* Vol. 1, *The Old River.* New York: Rinehart and Company, 1946.

Davis, William C. *Three Roads to the Alamo.* New York: HarperPerennial Edition, 1999.

———. *A Way through the Wilderness: The Natchez Trace and the Civilization of the Southern Frontier.* New York: HarperCollins Publishers, 1995.

Dow, Lorenzo. *History of Cosmopolite.* 5th ed. Wheeling, VA: Joshua Martin, 1848.

Dumont, Jean-Francois-Benjamin. *The Memoir of Lieutenant Dumont, 1715–1747: A Sojourner in the French Atlantic.* Chapel Hill: University of North Carolina Press, 2012.

Duncan, David Ewing. *Hernando de Soto: A Savage Quest in the Americas*. New York: Crown Publishers, 1995.

Feldman, Jay. *When The Mississippi Ran Backwards: Empire, Intrigue, Murder, and the New Madrid Earthquakes*. New York: Free Press, 2005.

Foreman, Josh, and Ryan Starrett. *Hidden History of Natchez*. Charleston, SC: The History Press, 2021.

Garcilaso de la Vega, the Inca. *La Florida*. Translated by Charmion Shelby and reprinted in *The De Soto Chronicles*. Tuscaloosa: University of Alabama Press, 1993.

Groom, Winston. *Vicksburg 1863*. New York: Vintage Civil War Library, 2009.

Guice, John D.W., ed. *By His Own Hand?: The Mysterious Death of Meriwether Lewis*. Norman: Oklahoma University Press, 2006.

Howard, H.R. *The History of Virgil A. Stewart*. Spartanburg, SC: Reprint Company, Publishers, 1976.

Hudson, Charles M. *Knights of Spain, Warriors of the Sun*. Athens: University of Georgia Press, 1997.

———. *The Southeastern Indians*. Knoxville: University of Tennessee Press, 1976.

Jenkins, Sally, and John Stauffer. *The State of Jones*. New York: Doubleday, 2009.

Judd, Naomi, with Marcia Wilkie. *River of Time: My Descent into Depression and How I Emerged with Hope*. New York: Hachette Book Group Inc., 2016.

King, Grace. *Jean Baptiste Le Moyne Sieur de Bienville*. London: Forgotten Books, 2018.

Lane, Mills. *Architecture of the Old South: Mississippi and Alabama*. Savannah, GA: Beehive Foundation, 1989.

Meachem, Jon. *American Lion: Andrew Jackson in the White House*. New York: Random House Trade Paperbacks, 2009.

Michener, James. *The Drifters*. New York: Random House Inc., 1971.

Myers, Kenneth M. *1729: The True Story of Pierre & Marie Mayeux, the Natchez Massacre and the Settlement of French Louisiana*. Denison, TX: Mayeux Press, 2017.

Pastwa, Agnes-Josephine. *Memoirs of My Life*. Translated by Pierre Clement de Laussat. Baton Rouge: Louisiana State University Press, 1978.

Payne-Gallwey, Sir Ralph. *The Crossbow, Mediæval and Modern, Military and Sporting*. London: Longmans, 1903.

Pénicaut. *Fleur de Lys and Calumet: Being the Penicaut Narrative of French Adventure in Louisiana*. Translated and edited by Richebourg Gaillard McWilliams. Tuscaloosa: University of Alabama Press, 1981.

Ramsey, James Gettys McReady. *The Annals of Tennessee to the End of the Eighteenth Century*. Charleston, SC: John Russell, 1853.

Rothert, Otto Arthur. *The Outlaws of Cave-in-Rock*. Cleveland, OH: Arthur H. Clark, 1924.

Schram, Pamela J., and Stephen G. Tibbetts. *Introduction to Criminology*. 3rd ed. Los Angeles, CA: Sage Publishing, 2012.

Shaffer, Lynda Norene. *Native Americans Before 1492*. New York: M.E. Sharpe, 1992.

Short Description of the Tennessee Government. Philadelphia, PA: Matthew Carey, 1793.

Turnbow, Tony L. *Hardened to Hickory: The Missing Chapter in Andrew Jackson's Life*. Nashville, TN: Tony L. Turnbow, 2018.

BIBLIOGRAPHY

Woodrick, Jim. *The Civil War Siege of Jackson Mississippi*. Charleston, SC: The History Press, 2016.

Wynne, Ben. *Mississippi's Civil War: A Narrative History*. Macon, GA: Mercer University Press, 2006.

Internet

Atlas Obscura. "Grave of Florence Irene Ford." https://www.atlasobscura.com/places/the-grave-of-florence-irene-ford.

Becherer, Max. "Photos: See Massive 12-Foot Long, 672-Pound Alligator Captured on the Pearl River." Nola.com, October 2, 2019. https://www.nola.com/multimedia/photos/collection_29e75bda-e56f-11e9-ae61-6f4bb8dae2d6.html#3.

Cisco, Jay Guy. *Historic Sumner County, TN*. 1909. http://sites.rootsweb.com/~tnsumner/gwinwm.htm.

Daniel, Jim. "Lewis County" TN Gen Web, September 16, 2019. https://tngenweb.org/lewis/robert-melville-cooper-of-lewis-county.

Elvispresleymusic.com.

Find a Grave. "Robert Theodore Cooper." https://www.findagrave.com/memorial/8845425/robert-theodore-cooper.

Frist, Bill. "Tennessee Is Home to One of the Deadliest Parks in the Nation: Here's How We Change That." *Forbes*, March 7, 2019. https://www.forbes.com/sites/billfrist/2019/03/07/tennessee-is-home-to-one-of-the-deadliest-national-parks-in-the-nation-heres-how-we-change-that/?sh=7571a4497d5e.

History.com. "Andrew Jackson Narrowly Escapes Assassination." https://www.history.com/this-day-in-history/andrew-jackson-narrowly-escapes-assassination.

Indiana Catholic History Web. "Father Senat Murdered." http://indianacatholic.mwweb.org/icath/?p=1155.

Issaquena County, Mississippi, History and Genealogy. http://genealogytrails.com/miss/issaquena/bios.html.

Lieb, Brad. "Battle of Ackia: Bienville Retreats." Chickasaw TV. https://www.chickasaw.tv/playlists/battle-of-ackia-videos/videos/battle-of-ackia-bienville-retreats.

Moore, Sue Burns. "Claiborne County, Mississippi and the Yellow Fever Epidemics." http://sites.rootsweb.com/~msclaib3/yellow1878.html.

———. "Death of General Lloyd Tilghman—The Legend of the 'Blood-Leaved Peach.'" The Battle of Champion Hill. battleofchampionhill.org.

National Park Service. "Mount Locust Inn Plantation." http://npshistory.com/brochures/natr/mount-locust-inn-plantation-2013.pdf.

———. "Rocky Springs Town Site, Milepost 54.8." https://www.nps.gov/places/rocky-springs-town-site.htm.

National Public Radio. "The Man Who Double-Crossed the Founders." April 28, 2010. https://www.npr.org/2010/04/28/126363998/the-man-who-double-crossed-the-founders.

Shelton, Lindsey. "Three Bites in Three Months, but Fewer Snakes?" *Natchez Democrat*, September 27, 2011. https://www.natchezdemocrat.com/2011/09/27/three-bites-in-three-months-but-fewer-snakes.

Tiede, Rachel. "Amid Recent Suicide Scares, Some Call for Temporary Solution on Natchez Trace Bridge." FOX-17, March 18, 2021. https://fox17.com/news/local/amid-recent-suicide-scares-some-call-for-temporary-solution-on-natchez-trace-bridge-williamson-county-tennessee.

Today in Mississippi. "Mississippi Seen: Vintage Shotgun a Tangible Connection to Legend." http://www.todayinmississippi.com/mississippi_seen/article/2911.

University of Florida, Department of Wildlife Ecology and Conservation. https://ufwildlife.ifas.ufl.edu/venomous_snake_faqs.shtml.

Williams, Angela. "Record Alligator Caught Near Natchez." WAPT. https://www.wapt.com/article/massive-alligators-caught-in-vicksburg/12106360.

Woodrick, Jim. "Lost in Flames: The Natchez Drug Company Explosion." *And Speaking of Which*, blog, October 18, 2013, http://andspeakingofwhich.blogspot.com/2013/10/lost-in-flames-natchez-drug-company.html.

Newspapers

Atlanta Constitution

Clarion and Tennessee State Gazette

Clarion-Ledger

Coffeeville Courier

Daily Journal

Detroit News

Enterprise-Journal (McComb, MS)

Evening Post (New York City)

Green's Impartial Observer

Greenwood Commonwealth

Mississippi Free Trader

Mississippi Messenger

Nashville Banner

Nashville Union and American

Natchez Democrat

Natchez Herald

Natchez Weekly Courier

New Orleans Crescent

New York Times

Port Gibson Herald

Star Herald (Kosciusko)

Tampa Bay Times

The Tennessean

Vicksburg Whig

Weekly Democrat (Natchez)

The World

Other

Kappler, Charles J., comp. and ed. "Treaty with the Chickasaw." *Indian Affairs: Laws and Treaties*. Vol. 2, *Treaties*. Washington, D.C.: Government Printing Office, 1904. Accessed through the Yale Law School website. https://avalon.law.yale.edu/18th_century/chic1786.asp.

Kitchin, Thomas, and T. Cadell. *Map of the European Settlements in North America*. [London?], 1776. Accessible via the Library of Congress. https://www.loc.gov/item/74692225.

"Letter to Union Chambers of Commerce, Washington Post. Signed by E. John Ellis, Louisiana, R.L. Gibson, Louisiana; John T. Morgan, Alabama; William H. McCardle, Mississippi; and Cyrus Bussey, president of the New Orleans Chamber of Commerce." September 9, 1878. In *Yellow Fever and Public Health in the New South*. Edited by John Ellis. Lexington: University Press of Kentucky, 1992.

Malone, James Henry. *The Chickasaw Nation*. Memphis Centenary Celebration, 1919.

National Park Service. National Register of Historic Places Registration Form: Emerald Mound. Digitized by the Mississippi Department of Archives and History (1988).

Regulations and Instructions Relating to His Majesty's Service at Sea. 9th ed. Privy Council, Great Britain, Admiralty. London, 1757.

"Strange Graves at Natchez City Cemetery" (Jerry Skinner Documentary). YouTube. https://www.youtube.com/watch?v=aml9PgV-SOw.

ABOUT THE AUTHORS

JOSH FOREMAN is from Jackson, Mississippi. His second home is Seoul, South Korea, where he lived, taught and traveled from 2005 to 2014. He holds degrees from Mississippi State University and the University of New Hampshire. He lives in Starkville, Mississippi, with his wife, Melissa, and his three children: Keeland, Genevieve and the soon-to-be-born child who, in late 2021, is being referred to as "Little Rupert." He teaches journalism at Mississippi State University.

RYAN STARRETT was birthed and reared in Jackson, Mississippi. After receiving degrees from the University of Dallas, Adams State University and Spring Hill College, as well as spending a ten-year hiatus in Texas, he has returned home to continue his teaching career. He lives in Madison with his wife, Jackie, and two children, Joseph Padraic and Penelope Rose.

CPSIA information can be obtained
at www.ICGtesting.com
Printed in the USA
LVHW081732290322
714728LV00003BA/123